Self-Esteem and the Physical You

Anita Canfield

Randall Publishers

ISBN No. 0-934126-21-6

First Printing, September, 1981

Randall Publishers
165 South Mountainway Drive
Suite 200
Orem, Utah 84057

Printed in the United States of America

ontents

Preface

Somewhere deep in the bosom of every woman is an *Eternal* burning, an *Eternal* longing to be feminine, to be lovely, to be honored and cherished. My heart aches for the women who have lost the spirit to rise to their election, the election of Goddess. Can you imagine a Goddess in any other way than feminine and clean and attractive?

My heart aches because I know how differently women would feel about themselves if they liked what they saw in the mirror. I know how much more productive women would be if they enjoyed their surroundings and felt peace there. I know how much more enthusiastic towards life and others women would be if they had more self-confidence, more self-esteem. I know how much liking the Physical You can mean in achieving greater self-confidence and love of self. I know how hard it is to invite the Spirit to dwell in your home when that home is dirty or unorganized. Without that Spirit there, it is almost impossible for a home to become a sanctuary, a refuge from the cares of the world, a place where self-discipline and self-esteem can be nurtured. And how do I know all that? I am a woman — no different from you.

I have suffered weight problems, appearance problems, acne, low income, and a poor self-image. Through years of trials and failures and successes I have come to an understanding of "who" must be involved in the "how" of gaining self-control and polishing self-esteem. The "who" is YOU, and the "how" is *gut-level labor*!

Design encompasses a sense of good taste and line. Whether in the home or on the body the same governing principles apply. The application of those principles, for someone who practices, can almost become a sixth sense. I want to share with you some of those design principles and ideas that will better your life.

Don't be frightened and think, "Oh, this will be for Francine Fashion Model or Dolly Designer. I'm just Priscilla Plain Jane, and I can't ever be like that." Those are self-defeating attitudes. What is written in this book is not for models or design students. It is for wives, mothers, single women, and widows. It is for any woman who is a homemaker, regardless of whether or not she has a family.

This is a book about basics. After you practice basics, something surprising will happen. ONCE BASICS HAVE BECOME "FAMILIAR" TO YOU, YOU CAN BE MORE CREATIVE. By studying and applying the simple basics to your life and practicing them, you will become more creative in even the routine areas.

There are two parts to this book. Part One deals with the Physical You as it relates to your health, body, and appearance. Part Two deals with the Physical You as it relates to your home, cleanliness, privacy, and budget decorating.

I must give heartfelt thanks here to two women who helped me with the grooming section. Miss Sharon Norman, owner of the Mane Production in Las Vegas, is a talented cosmetologist. She has built a prestigious beauty salon and clientele in a few short years because of her talents and expertise in coiffures and make-up techniques. She has also won numerous awards. Mrs. Bernie Lenz, also an award winner, owns Fashion Merchandising Institute of Nevada, is a wife, mother, and homemaker who has put lots of glamour into her life and the lives of others by her expert instruction in fashion, the body, and personal appearance.

I also wish to thank Dr. S. Scott Zimmerman, a professor of biochemistry at Brigham Young University, who contributed an outstanding review of his work regarding obesity and endurance exercise. Dr. Zimmerman is married, the father of six children, and has personally lost over forty pounds by following his program. I would like to thank, too, all my clients who graciously allowed me to use the photographs of their homes. Also, thanks to my associates and friends who volunteered their time and talents to me — Joann Evans, Lynn White, Candy Krausman, Theresa Hollingsworth, and Devra Hollis. A very special thank you to my sister, Renee McCormick, for being such a great help and to Steve for his meticulous design of the covers of my books.

To include all the information available on the two subjects covered in this book would have produced a thick-volumned index. That's not the idea. You wouldn't want to read an index anyway. I have condensed and compiled philosophies, guidelines, and ideas into (1) simple language, (2) techniques the average woman can apply on a daily basis, (3) ideas that require a minimum amount of effort for the end result, and (4) affordable ideas and plans. This book is concise and meant to inspire you to practice the basics and to make *simple* changes. Once you master those basics, you will begin to develop the ability to experiment and create. While reading this, take a colored marking pencil and mark the lines or pages that apply to you or that impress you the most. It will make it easy to refer to them on a daily basis.

Life styles change, clothes and fashions change, seasonal colors and fabrics and furniture change, but in the words of writer Jobyna Ralston, "There are a few things that never go out of style, and a feminine woman is one of them." The poet Shelley called woman the most delightful of all God's creations, for "she is the most delightful of God's creatures — Heaven's best gift — man's joy and pride in posterity and his support and comfort in affliction.''

Lovely women, the Lord made you to temper man, to succor the child, to inspire poets, to teach compassion, to let the world believe in heaven. You have amazing brightness, purity, truth, eternal joy, and everlasting love. It has been said that a woman has more strength in her looks than does a court of law. I have noticed that those women who have a command of their appearance and their homes do have a greater influence over others. Have you ever noticed that there are only two kinds of women in the world as far as appearance goes? There are those who are plain and those who are colorful.

Somewhere deep in the bosom of every woman is that *Eternal* burning, that *Eternal* longing to be feminine, to be lovely, to be honored for her beauty and her home. Those longings are there because women are sensing a former sphere and existence where there was a house of love and order, a school, a place of beauty, a sanctuary. And the Woman who presided over it? She taught us what it was to be a woman. She was more than we can ever imagine — so much more. We must rise to that election.

Part One

Chapter  One

The Crown Jewels

"Every action of our lives touches on some chord that will vibrate in eternity."

—E. H. Chapin

As I sat in a hospital waiting room some months ago, I saw a woman who broke my heart. She was about fifty years old and fifty pounds overweight. Her hair was dirty, and although gray, it was streaked with yellow. It was stringy and hung about her shoulders where it separated into wide, greasy strands. Her face was puffy and pock-marked, and her nose and eyelids seemed almost swollen. She wore a man's tee shirt, and rolled up in one sleeve was a package of cigarettes. She had on skin-tight, black pedal pushers, and her unshaven legs bulged from the bottom of those pants. She had maneuvered a sand-filled smoker in front of the small sofa where she sat smoking one cigarette after another. She was sitting with her legs apart, her belly protruding between her legs. She wore no bra, was hunched over, and smoked and puffed with great vigor.

I was overwhelmed. Where had she come from? Who was she? Didn't she care what she looked like? Where was her femininity? Didn't anybody care? No, no one cared. She didn't even care. Hadn't she once been a little rosy-cheeked, golden-haired toddler? Had she once had dreams of sweet sixteen? My heart ached for her as I thought of my own sweet little nine-year-old daughter asking me if she were old enough for panty hose. I wanted to run over to that woman, throw my arms around her repulsive countenance, and tell her that I cared, that I loved her, and knew what kind of woman God wanted her to be. To see a sister like that broke my heart. She had let herself go to pieces, and she didn't even care. She had abused her body in every sense of the word. She had lost all her sense of womanly nature.

I often hear my husband or brothers discuss with their friends an old flame or a female acquaintance and comment that "she'd really let herself go." Of course, I'm sure it was never to the extreme of the poor creature I saw in the hospital waiting room, but there had been enough of a change in the physical appearance that it caused a remark or two.

What happens to us in life? What happens to that rosy-cheeked, sparkling-eyed, neatly-coiffed darling of five, of ten, or nineteen, so full of wonder and hope and the promises of a life ahead, a future with Mr. Wonderful, and the cottage by the edge of the woods? We marry and then move into the trailer park, or apartment building, or tract home, and nine months from the wedding day we're a new mother with ten or twenty extra pounds to lose. Is that when we lose the lustre, when the reality sets in?

Maybe we don't marry. Friends pass us by and send cards and birth announcements. Dating turns into a routine, or worse, into disasters. It's easier to stay home, fix a plate of brownies, and crochet Christmas presents or curl up with a good book. Is that when we begin to fade into wallflowers, when the reality sets in?

Maybe we think no one else cares either. A friend went shopping and bought herself a whole new wardrobe. She had looked tired and worn and plain for too long, and she knew it. A new hairstyle, new clothes, a lesson in make-up application, and she was radiant. Her step seemed a little lighter, and she told me she felt like a new person. She was lovely, but her husband didn't acknowledge her change, said he didn't care, and a neighbor lady even teased her. She was devastated. She felt that if no one else cared, she wouldn't either. Is that when we lose the sparkle, when the reality sets in?

It isn't that Latter-day Saint women are fatter or frumpier than non-member women. However, Latter-day Saint women are busy all week filling their lives with families, church activities, caring and compassionate service, missionary work and genealogy, and civic responsibilities. Visiting teaching alone can require many hours in a month. Saturdays are spent preparing for the Sabbath, and the Sabbath is kept holy. Pressure, pressure, pressure!

Non-member women, as a general rule, don't have these kinds of selfless activities, so they fill their time with more self-centered pursuits such as sports, shopping, health clubs, fashion shows, Sunday recreation, and so on. Not knowing or understanding the will of the Lord, they occupy their thoughts with the things of the world, and rightly so, as they know no other way. They are good women, and many are waiting to hear the gospel. From whom will they hear it? From YOU, their neighbor, fellow P.T.A. member, door-to-door cosmetic representative, or fellow employee. They see you, and they see a Latter-day Saint woman. It is only after someone is seen that they are heard. It's disheartening when the appearance doesn't match the voice.

I am not making excuses for Latter-day Saint women by inferring that they often let their appearances or homes slide below a high standard because they are in active pursuit of the Lord's work. And MAKE NO MISTAKE, I am not advocating that we all run out and concern ourselves only with clothes, make-up, and nice furniture. There is a happy medium. You must first be endeavoring to serve the Lord. You must first be filling your lives with what He wants you to do, but you MUST also be concerned with HOW you are doing it. Part of the HOW is your appearance. It distresses me to hear women say they have more important things to do, for I am certain that if I were a non-member vascillating between a No-ERA vote and a YES-ERA vote, and a nice, but dowdy, seemingly repressed, and behind-the-times Mormon neighbor tried to convince me to vote against the ERA, I would not be very persuaded. No matter how sound her argument was, if she didn't look like a confident woman, she would not be very convincing.

APPEARANCES DO COUNT. Can you imagine Sister Barbara Smith wearing a long, flowering mumu with puffy sleeves, about fifty pounds overweight, and wearing no make-up to appear on national television opposite an ERA proponent? Can you imagine President Kimball coming home to a fungus-infested refrigerator, stained carpets, and greasy sinks? Can you imagine a wife of one of the General Authorities allowing her family to sleep between soiled sheets or to comb their hair in front of a sticky mirror? Of course, not. It's so out of character. Ah, that's the word! Character!

"CHARACTER IS EDUCATED WILL." Character is built out of mental attitude and action. The mental attitude must be the knowledge of who you are. It is believing in yourself. It is positive thinking. The action is the will, the desire, the moving forward to accomplish. You cannot dream about forming character, it is something you must mold and shape and forge for yourself. With exactly the same materials, one woman will build a palace while another builds a hovel.

I've heard all the excuses. I've even used some from time to time.

"I don't have time. I have more important things to do." I wonder what would happen to our missionary force if they all said that? They certainly have important things to do, and yet they are required to keep themselves well-groomed.

"I don't want to be vain." Why do so many people think that to look nice, you must be trying to impress others? Is it possible to want to look nice for yourself so that you will feel better about yourself? I wonder who Sister Kimball is trying to impress? She always looks so lovely.

"I am concerning myself with spiritual matters." The Lord mentioned something about that in the scriptures, didn't He? I believe He said that all things to Him are spiritual. There is not a more spiritual thing on earth for each of us personally than our bodies and our homes.

Have you ever said any of these things to yourself before? What is an excuse anyway? Isn't it a lack of honesty with self as well as a lack of self-discipline? It's a way of justifying what you shouldn't be doing or neglecting. In seeking feedback for my first book, I prepared a questionnaire for women about self-esteem. Some of the questions dealt with physical appearance. Out of the questionnaires returned, most women said they were overweight. ALL of them said they weren't satisfied with their physical appearance and wished they could be more attractive. Is this desire for attractiveness and femininity a false desire propagated by the fashion and cosmetic industries? Is it the product of an environment which emphasizes carnal lusts and vanity? Some people may believe that this desire in women stems from such causes, but I am not one who does.

A lovely young woman came to me for help. She just wasn't happy, and she wanted to feel better about herself. We eventually discussed her appearance. She was overweight and sloppy. Her apartment was just plain dirty. She hadn't been concerned about those things because she said she was only concerned with the spiritual development of her self-esteem. I explained that the two can't be separated. God cannot dwell in an unclean home, nor can the spirit shine out of a careless body.

"That's fine for some people but not for me," she said. *"I'm just not the type."*

"Do you know you are a daughter of God?" I asked.

"Yes," she said.

"Do you really KNOW it?"

"I think so."

"I don't mean think. Do you KNOW?"

"I hope so," she said.

"No, not hope," I insisted. "Do you KNOW it?"

She finally admitted that she didn't. THAT WAS HER PROBLEM. I knew that she didn't really know it, or she wouldn't have felt the way she did about herself. She was struggling for spiritual identity, and she felt that if she gained that, she would be free of the feelings of worthlessness which plagued her. She was only partly right.

When you know who you are, when you know who taught you first, you realize that not to respect your body and environment is not to respect those who taught you.

DO YOU KNOW WHO YOU ARE?

I have an imaginary photograph of my former life. There I see myself as an infant, nurtured in the arms of a heavenly mother. As a young child caressed in the arms of heavenly parents, taught at the knees of those heavenly parents, and, when it was my turn, hugged good-bye by those heavenly parents. I know they love me because I am theirs. I KNOW WHO I AM. Before I left, they taught me well.

I'm certain my mother there was my strongest teacher and influence. How do I know what she taught when the veil has been so tightly drawn? Deep within my bosom, deep in the lifeblood coursing through me, there is a spark of remembrance.

Let's call it a longing, a longing to be like her, to emulate her, to remember what she taught. How else do you explain those feelings women have, that sixth sense toward femininity? It is a longing to be lovely, to be feminine, *a longing to be like her*. I have a mental picture of her, and although I see no exact features, hair color, or height, I do see grace, elegance, self-control, perfect form, cleanliness, purity, and goddess-like femininity. Can you imagine her as being any other way?

Who are you kidding when you say you don't care about your physical appearance or your home? You are kidding only yourself, or else you are denying that remembrance planted deep in your bosom. You are choking your character.

I'm sure these were the things a mother in heaven taught us. It was a huge responsibility. We saw her, too. She was a visual example to us. I think there will be no greater shock to any of us than when we pass through the veil and see how well we did know our heavenly parents and how much they did teach us.

As women of the Lord's true Church, we belong to an elect group — better than the Ladies Garden Club or the American Revolutionary Bluebloods. We are the BLUEBLOOD women of the earth. If we have such an important message to declare and such serious stands to take, ought we not look like we belong to such an elect group?

I enjoy reading the description Josephus gives of the Savior when He was on the earth. He wore the robes and sandals of the day and even His beard was combed and styled in the fashion of His day and custom. He knew it was important to go out among the people and not only look like He was the Son of God, but look like He had something important to say. The appearance of the Prophet and General Authorities is dignified, prestigious, and modern.

It is a serious mistake to think that the way we look or live does not influence or affect others as well as ourselves. It does. I see obese parents rearing obese children. I see sloppy women with sloppy husbands and disheveled children. I see my own children picking up some of my own negative responses. What we are does influence others. We must make ourselves a light to the world. It IS important what others think of us. If we are to do good, we must not only be tactful and loving, we must look like we know WHO WE ARE — THE WOMEN OF GOD.

So maybe you know all this, but getting the job done is another story you say. I love the prophet Alma. In that part of the *Book of Mormon* there are so many instructions for just plain daily living. He talks about all those things we have to do that perhaps aren't easy or pleasant. He calls it giving place:

> Now, as I said concerning faith — that it was not a perfect knowledge — even so it is with my words. Ye cannot know of their surety at first, unto perfection, any more than faith is a perfect knowledge. But behold, if ye will *awake* and arouse your faculties, even to an experiment upon my words, and exercise a particle of faith, yea, even if ye can no more than desire to believe, let this desire work in you, even until ye believe in a manner that ye can *give place* for a portion of my words. (Alma 32:26-27. Italics added.)

First, you must awake and have a goal, then a willingness to TRY. To give place is a willingness to change, perhaps to do a lot of changing!

When we were in England, we went to the Tower of London to see the Crown Jewels. They were magnificent. There were several crowns of solid gold set with huge diamonds, emeralds, rubies, and sapphires. There was an orb made of solid gold, and swords, rings, bracelets, and goblets also encrusted with jewels. The most fabulous piece was the sceptre, set with a 530-carat diamond.

I have never seen such perfection, such beauty, such brilliance in any other precious stones. We have toured many museums both in Europe and America and have seen a lot of gems, yet these were the most beautiful ever. The size, the cut, the clarity were dazzling. Rare, and almost sacred, England cherishes them and guards them with great care. As we left the Tower, I reflected on how exciting it would be to wear them for just a night! Then I slowly began to think about my own crown jewels, precious jewels that I can wear everyday. They are more rare than any stones. The size, cuts, and clarity are entirely up to me. They are jewels that are to be cherished and guarded with great care. They are faith, obedience, prayer, repentance, and the 530-carat jewel is self-discipline. They are set in pure, 24-carat love — love of God for me, my love of the gospel, and love of myself. Those crown jewels must be worn each day in order for me to "give place" and find true love of self.

Exercising self-discipline is not only a matter of strength but endurance. It is worth noting what the Duke of Wellington said concerning the British and the Battle of Waterloo: "The British were not braver than the French, they were only brave five minutes longer." And that is what it takes from you, just a little more discipline than you have had in the past. Just a little more commitment than you have given before. It means *giving place longer.*

Let me share with you the story of a teenager's failure and then eventual success. It was a simple problem but a crippling one: profanity. During the baptismal interview, the bishop, who was aware of the problem, asked the soon-to-be member if a goal to curb this degrading problem could be realized. He challenged the young man to overcome this bad habit within one year from the baptismal date.

The baptism was in March. During that month the new

member set a goal to be consciously aware of profanity and challenged himself to say no more than twelve profane words, an even dozen during the month of March. Each month thereafter he would simply eliminate one more word until the goal was realized.

He kept a close tabulation and accounted for each slip. About the middle of March he was already up to ten and so agonized for the last two weeks of the month, biting his tongue and clinching his teeth, but he made it with a cool twelve. In April he went down to eleven, in May ten, nine in June, and eight in July. All was going well, and he was feeling great self-esteem. Then something happened — stress, pressure, whatever — and in August he slipped. He tallied up twelve lapses and so was back where he had started!

Oh, how often when we try and try and then fail, we just quit. We become subject to frustration and Satan's discouragement and our own weaknesses. This young man could have done that. He felt horrible. Don't you when you slide back? Nevertheless, he had made a commitment. He had to keep trying. He did, and in September he only slipped four times! One year later he had conquered the problem. If he had given up in the blackness of August, he would have never known the ecstasy of September.

OH, IF WE COULD ONLY OVERCOME THE AUGUSTS OF OUR LIVES!

Ask yourself these questions: Are there problems like weight control, self-control, cleanliness, and grooming on the other side of the veil? Do you think we can procrastinate the day of self-control? Do you think that if our time is cut short, we can go to the other side of the veil free from our weaknesses?

Consider what Alma had to say on this subject:

> For behold, this life is the time for men to
> prepare to meet God; yea, behold the day of this
> life is the day for men to perform their labors.
>
> And now, as I said unto you before, as ye

have had so many witnesses, therefore, I beseech of you that ye do not procrastinate the day of your repentance until the end; for after this day of life, which is given us to prepare for eternity, behold, if we do not improve our time while in this life, then cometh the night of darkness wherein there can be no labor performed.

Ye cannot say, when ye are brought to that awful crisis, that I will repent, that I will return to my God. Nay, ye cannot say this; for that same spirit which doth possess your bodies at the time that ye go out of this life, that same spirit will have power to possess your body in that eternal world. (Alma 34:32-34.)

I believe that Alma was talking about anything and everything that is offensive to God. When we abuse our minds, our bodies, or our homes, we offend God. Now is the day to prepare to meet Him. Now, because tomorrow we may be there. And when we go, what then? Alma tells us that "if we do not improve our time while in this life, then cometh the night of darkness . . . for that same spirit which doth possess your bodies at the time that ye go out of this life, that same spirit will have power to possess your body in that eternal world." Notice that Alma said BODY. Could it mean that we carry our weaknesses over the veil and into immortality? If you have a problem with self-control in this world, does it simply leave you in the next? If you have a problem in this life, are you going to be able to solve it in the next?

WE HAVE TO OVERCOME OUR WEAKNESSES either in this life or the next. The Lord expects us to do so, but how long will it take if we wait to do so in the next life? A lot of people will be absolutely startled when they cross that veil and find out that they are the same person with the same things to overcome.

When I think about all the weaknesses I will probably carry with me, it makes me want to get rid of them as fast as I can!

Even if you say you've tried and failed, you must keep trying. It is not so important WHERE you are but in what DIRECTION you are going. Each day conquered here is a day subtracted there! Failure is a part of growing. You can overcome your failures. If you fail at something, it does not mean you are a failure. You ARE a failure if you never try or if, in trying, you give up.

Now some of you sisters have handicaps. Mortality seems unfair to everyone. We look toward eternity with the hope of justice, but, here and now, do you look to those handicaps as an excuse to settle back into the complacency and comfort of frumpiness? Or worse, do you think you are unattractive and worthless because of your physical impairment?

I love Helen Keller. I wish she were alive now. I would find a way to meet her. When I get over to the other side, she's one of the people on my list that I am going to look up. She should be an inspiration to women everywhere, handicapped either physically or by their own weaknesses! Inspiration is the wrong word to describe her. She is a ROCK. I love her because of her life. What prompted my interest in Helen Keller was a picture of her in the encyclopedia. When I saw it, I was astonished by the look on her face. She did not look blind. There was a definite sparkle in her eyes, a look of depth, intelligence, and recognition. Eyes are the reflection of the soul. Every ounce of her soul was reflected in her eyes and in her whole face. As I read books about her work and thoughts and accomplishments, I felt her indomitable spirit, her enthusiasm for life, her refusal to let her handicaps affect her stay on earth. She was responsible for much of the improvement of life for the blind. She graduated from Radcliffe with honors. She was active on the staffs of many foundations for the blind and deaf. She travelled to underdeveloped and war-ravaged countries and helped establish better conditions there for the blind. She

14

lectured in America and in twenty-five other countries. She aided and comforted servicemen who had been blinded in World War II. She wrote many books which have been translated into more than fifty languages. Wherever she went, she brought new courage to thousands of blind persons and inspired millions of others with her zeal. She never married, she never had any children, but she influenced literally millions. She could have said, "I'm blind, I'm deaf, I'm dumb, who will listen to me? Who can I help? What do I care how I love or look or act?" But no! She said just the opposite, and after she had said it, she lived it! }

Harry Emerson Fosdick attended a concert by a great violinist at Carnegie Hall. During that concert the violinist's "A" string snapped, but he went on to finish the concert on three strings. Afterwards at a gathering, someone was heard to philosophize: "Well, that's life, to have your "A" string snap and finish on three." Mr. Fosdick reflected for a moment and then said, "*No*, that is not merely life, that is life VICTORIOUS!"

That's life for us, as God's daughters, to take whatever comes after the "A" string snaps and finish victoriously. You can do it! You are one of His daughters. You possess, if in embryo, every attribute possessed by God himself. You have the power within you. That word POWER is a literal word meaning the ability to act, to produce, and to effect.

Late one night I was writing down some thoughts about the POWER of positive thinking. A lot has been said and written about that subject, and I felt well versed and well read on the matter. I finished writing and went to bed. At about 5:00 the next morning, I woke up almost startled with the impression that I should read in the *Book of Moses*. I began with the first verse of the first chapter. In the fourth chapter I came upon the description of the Lord casting Satan from the Garden of Eden: "And I will put enmity between thee and the woman, between thy seed and her seed; and he (mankind) shall bruise thy head, and thou (Satan) shalt bruise his heel." (Moses 4:21.)

Satan has a POWER over us, the power of negative thinking. Nevertheless, it is a POWER less than the POWER given to the seed of Adam — all mankind. The POWER to bruise the head is far greater than the POWER to bruise the heel. There in that garden scene the Lord gave mankind this greater POWER and control over the body.

We women marvel at PRIESTHOOD POWER and stand in awe of miracles commanded by that ability to act in God's name. Realize that you have been given a POWER by which to govern your own thoughts, a power whereby your spirit may control your body. And the spirit must control the body for self-esteem to develop.

An obese woman told me she knew her body was overfed because her spirit was underfed. When you feed the spirit, the spirit controls the body. The two are inseparable. Why else does the Lord give us commandments to clean up our homes, get enough rest, eat properly, do all things in moderation, study the scriptures, pray constantly, and live by the Spirit?

While we tend to look at the commandments and admonitions we are given and consider some more spiritual, and hence more important, we should remember what the Lord has said of his commandments:

> Wherefore, verily I say unto you that all things unto me are spiritual, and not at any time have I given unto you a law which was temporal; neither any man, nor the children of men; neither Adam, your father, whom I created.
>
> Behold, I gave unto him that he should be an agent unto himself; and I gave unto him commandment, but no temporal commandment gave I unto him, for my commandments are spiritual; they are not natural nor temporal, neither carnal nor sensual. (D&C, 29:34-35.)

We have also been commanded:

Organize yourselves; prepare every needful thing; and establish a house, even a house of prayer, a house of fasting, a house of faith, a house of learning, a house of glory, a house of order, a house of God;

That your incomings may be in the name of the Lord; that your outgoings may be in the name of the Lord; that all your salutations may be in the name of the Lord, with uplifted hands unto the Most High . . . .

Cease to be idle; cease to be unclean; cease to find fault one with another; cease to sleep longer than is needful; retire to thy bed early, that ye may not be weary; arise early, that your bodies and your minds may be invigorated. (D&C 88:119-120, 124.)

If you know WHO you are and then EXERCISE that POWER given to you, you will be able to conquer any mountain — indeed mountain range — of obstacles. Remember that the woman at the top of the mountain didn't *fall* there!

Self-control comes with practice, and with increased practice comes mastery. Self-control used once swells a person's heart with self-respect (self-esteem). I DID IT! You can actually say that to yourself. I DID IT. ONCE is the beginning of that self-respect which motivates you to succeed a second time. Two successes stimulate desire for a third, and so on until control comes out of self-respect and self-respect comes from self-control.

My three-year-old son stayed by my side for three hours one Thanksgiving Eve. He stood vigil and "helped" me make twelve apple pies. His unwavering concentration amazed me. He was fascinated (so was I — at his delight in the entire task.) He was so enthused that he wanted me to call everyone he knew and tell

17

them the good news that he had helped make all the pies for dinner. He wanted to put them in the oven, and he wanted to take them out. He wanted to watch them cool off, and then he wanted the first taste. I went to bed that night seeing his enraptured expressions. Thanksgiving Day was nice, and I all but forgot the ache in my legs and hands from the labor of twelve pies. The following morning I was preparing to leave the house, and it occurred to me that Chase was being very quiet — *too* quiet. As I entered the kitchen, there was a trail of flour from my baking drawer to his oatmeal bowl. As my eyes focused, I saw the real mess: oatmeal, flour, eggs from the refrigerator (cracked shells and all), pepper, salt, sugar, and who knows what else in the dozen pie pans that lay on the table, the sink, and the floor! My first reaction was to run for the razor blades (for my wrists, not his). Then came the second reaction as a full wave of anger swept over me. I started across the kitchen to get the wooden spoon that was soon to meet a little boy's bottom.

I had been praying for several weeks that I might be more patient with my children. I soon came to understand how prayers work. If you want wisdom, the Lord blesses you with problems. If you want courage, he gives you trials. I was almost ready to quit praying for patience! I was ready to tell Him that I had changed my mind and didn't want patience after all. My children had been unusually trying ever since I had been praying for patience!

As I started across the kitchen, another spirit seemed to overwhelm me. I stopped.

"Now someday," it said to me, "you will tell him about this, and you'll both laugh. Why not enjoy him now, too?"

I stood there, disbelieving my own CALM thoughts. Then I recognized that the calmness had come from the Holy Ghost. Sure, I had to be firm and explain to Chase about the mess (Oh, what a mess!) and why he couldn't yet make a pie by himself, but

I did it with a whole new attitude, one that has changed my life.

He helped me clean up the sticky pans and the floor. As we were finishing, he came over and threw his arms around my neck, looked up at me with big brown eyes, and said, "I'm so sorry, Mommy." If I had not listened to the Spirit, I would have missed that sweet moment.

Worse yet, I would have missed a great lesson in self-control. The experience lingered on in my thoughts all that day. Then suddenly I said, almost aloud, I DID IT! I was patient in the midst of chaos. I did it! That experience brought all my prayer to *real light*. It brought new hope for my supplication to the Lord. It brought me a tremendous feeling of self-control and self-respect. I did it once, and I could do it again! The hard part had been that first step toward tasting the sweetness of success. *Self-control sparks self-esteem, and renewed self-esteem encourages more self-control.*

In the *Ensign Magazine* (March, 1980, page 29), there is a story written by a woman who had had a similar experience:

> I had been trying to diet for several weeks but kept putting it off. Besides, the cookie jar was still half full of gooey, chocolate chip cookies. I'll diet after these cookies are gone, I said to myself.
>
> But when I finally did reach for a cookie, I changed my mind and closed the cupboard door. At that moment I made a conscious choice to eat an apple instead — a small decision, but a decision nevertheless. The apple was crisp and delicious. And my small decision to eat that apple gave me the self-esteem I needed to again use self-control: at lunch I ate a salad. For the rest of the day I ate vegetables and fruits rich in vitamins and low in calories. By the end

of the day I felt elated; I had actually done it — I had dieted for one full day!

Goals can be reached by one small step or one small choice at a time. Each step becomes easier because of the self-esteem and faith gained at the last step.

I *loved* her use of the term "conscious choice." You will never do anything you don't consciously think about. You will never become anything you don't ponder in your heart. As a woman thinketh, so is she. If you don't consciously think about self-improvement, you will never improve. If you don't consciously choose to lose weight or clean your home, you never will. The choice is literally up to you.

The Holy Ghost plays an active role in our self-discipline. He is not a passive member of the Godhead, and He is there to first help us see our weaknesses and then inspire and aid us in conquering them. The scripture says: "For of him unto whom much is given much is required" (D&C 82:3), but I believe that holds true in reverse — where you have required more of yourself, the Lord gives you a great deal back. That is true of tithing and time and all sacrifices. It is most true of self-discipline. It is a measure between you and the Lord alone. If you have put in the level of labor through PRAYER and ACTION, He will see that you are uplifted, inspired, and spiritually renewed.

You will not, however, be guaranteed freedom from discomfort or from Satan's antagonism. During the month prior to a particular Spiritual Living lesson, I made an assignment to several sisters to exercise self-control in certain areas. They were to report the results of their experience to me before the coming lesson. As each sister reported, each had gained something different out of the assignment. Each had focused on her own special needs. But a most interesting fact became apparent as each sister discussed her activity. Without exception they all said that they had felt a dark spirit brooding over them while they had been trying to control thoughts, actions, appetites, etc. The harder they had tried, the stronger that influence had become. They all sensed Satan's interference. In spite of this, they had been able to succeed in carrying out the assignment.).

After the reports came in, I remembered a special chapter in the *Book of Mormon*. It is a comforting scripture that I have come to love. In Third Nephi we are told that the prophet Nephi, upon seeing the wickedness of his people, cried to the Lord all day that He might preserve the people and not destroy them: "Now it came to pass that when Nephi, the son of Nephi, saw this wickedness of his people, his heart was exceedingly sorrowful.

"And it came to pass that he went out and bowed himself down upon the earth, and cried mightily to his God in behalf of his people, yea, those who were about to be destroyed because of their faith in the tradition of their fathers.

"And it came to pass that he cried mightily unto the Lord, all the day." (3 Nephi 1:10-12).

The Lord accepted this great prophet's tender prayer, told him to be of good cheer, and assured him that He would give the people a sign that very night, for it was the eve of His birth: "Behold, the voice of the Lord came unto him, saying: Lift up your head and be of good cheer; for behold, the time is at hand, and on this night shall the sign be given, and on the morrow come I into the world, to show unto the world that I will fulfill all that which I have caused to be spoken by the mouth of my holy prophets" (3 Nephi 1:12-13).

The sign was given, and the people were astonished. They had heard the words of the prophets for many years and had failed to heed them. At the appearance of the sign, their hearts turned to the Lord, and the people fell to their knees and repented:

For behold, at the going down of the sun

there was no darkness; and the people began to be astonished because there was no darkness when the night came.

And there were many, who had not believed the words of the prophets, who fell to the earth and became as if they were dead, for they knew that the great plan of destruction . . . had been frustrated; for the signal which had been given was already at hand.

. . . All the people upon the face of the whole earth from the west to the east, both in the land north and in the land south, were so exceedingly astonished that they fell to the earth.

For they knew that the prophets had testified of these things for many years, and that the sign which had been given was already at hand; and they began to fear because of their iniquity and their unbelief. (3 Nephi 1:15-18.)

As the people repented, there was an outpouring of the Spirit. The people had broken hearts and contrite spirits. They desired to be better. They were intent on abiding by the instructions of the prophets. Nevertheless, as soon as they began to *give place,* they also experienced an outpouring from Satan: "And it came to pass that *from this time forth* there began to be lyings sent forth among the people, by Satan, to harden their hearts, to the intent that they might not believe in those signs and wonders which they had seen; *but notwithstanding these lyings and deceivings the more part of the people did believe, and were converted unto the Lord"* (3 Nephi 1:22, italics added).

Whenever there is an increased effort to obtain the spirit,

there is an increased force opposing such an effort. Nevertheless, we can rise above such opposition and succeed. Even in the depths of discouragement, even in the black hole of despair, you can see a light if you focus clearly. Focus on positive thoughts, on commitment, on the Savior. Focus clearly on the most positive thought you have have: THE LORD AND I CONSTITUTE A MAJORITY.

Satan will really pour out his heinous vile over you. He'll really pour it on thick, but just look over your shoulders and say to him: "Well, you really blew it! You really overdid it! If you had just poured out a small dose, you might have won, but when the opposition is so strong, I KNOW my decisions and actions are right!"

A noted photographer once explained the secret of his ability to capture the personalities of the famous women he photographed. He said he was able to make each woman appear so beautiful and unique because he made each believe that she was the most beautiful woman on earth. Hours before each session he would talk to them, tell them how beautiful they should feel, and have them say over and over out loud, "I am beautiful." While he photographed, he would ask each woman to concentrate on her *inner* qualities, her *inner* beauty. She might go over and over in her mind what a beautiful smile she had or how lovely her compassion was or how much love she had for her family. She might contemplate her patience, chastity, dignity, or whatever she felt was an inner quality.

He had each woman concentrate on this idea and at the same time consider themselves to be THE most beautiful woman on earth. He would tell them that they were lovely, exquisite, etc. He would talk about their most expressive features and give sincere compliments. He explained that he believed that every woman's inner beauty could make her outwardly beautiful. He proved his point. He won award after award for capturing "the soul of a woman." He became famous for his "Beautiful

Women." They were not all movie queens. Some were quite plain, but his secret was mind over matter, a positive mental attitude, the POWER of positive thinking — as a woman thinketh, so is she!

It is not important to be as physically beautiful as THE most beautiful woman on earth. Beauty is in the eye of the beholder. A resurrected being is so glorious, so exquisitely beautiful, so unlike anything we have ever seen. The Prophet Joseph Smith had a difficult time describing such things.

The point is, you are what you think. Negative thoughts can only cripple your self-esteem. "I can't do it. I just can't lose this weight. My house is a shack. I'm a plain Jane. This apartment is dumpy. My hips are too big. This furniture is just second hand junk. My deformity makes me ugly. I can't give up sweets." You can change such thoughts as these. *You can if you will to do!*

These are some of the basic principles which you must keep in mind as you strive to lift your thinking and make a better, *happier* you:

1. Understand WHO YOU ARE and who taught you how to be a woman.
2. Cleanliness and personal beauty of body and home are godlike qualities stemming from character and reverence.
3. Your circle of influence increases as your physical beauty begins to match your spiritual beauty.
4. You have been given a great POWER, the POWER of positive mental attitude.
5. With that mental power, you can ACT.
6. ACTION is a result of self-discipline.
7. All of the above produce CHARACTER, educated will.
8. Strong character and godlike character

produce a solid and healthy self-esteem.
9.   You must endure to the end of your life.

For the Latter-day Saint woman, self-esteem is cradled and nurtured in the arms of gospel principles. To achieve self-esteem, we must, as Paul declared, "press toward the mark for the prize of the high calling of God in Christ Jesus" (Philippians 3:14). That prize is so extraordinary, so delicious to our senses that Satan is relentless in his attacks on our self-esteem. That is the only way he knows how to win. The spiritual development of each woman's mind will cause her to rise up and never be the same again. The PARTNER to that inward development is the outward development. The inside can't fully sparkle when the outside is tarnished.

The Lord has given us these tabernacles of clay and commanded us to care for them. Likewise, He has given us our homes and possessions to care for. He *expects* us to do just that.

I love the chapters in Mosiah where King Benjamin is addressing the people. He preaches the gospel and bears his testimony so eloquently. He must have been so powerful and so full of the Spirit. Then, after hours of poignant speech, he drew to the close of his sermon with a simple statement, the key to it all: "And now, if you believe all these things see that ye *do* them" (Mosiah 4:10, italics added).

Real femininity has nothing to do with lipstick, pattern, lace, color, ruffles, and frills. Although those things will enhance femininity, real femininity IS AN ATTITUDE. It is an awareness of the role of godhood. It doesn't take away from your capabilities. Femininity is a natural or God-given characteristic. The gospel teaches us the differences between man and woman. These differences are meant to make men and women dependent upon each other. Femininity then, is the other half of godhood.

If you believe in the woman God intends for you to be, you

25

will rise up and never be the same again. I love you. I believe in you. I know you can do it.

Yours is an election, and you must rise to that election.

Chapter  Two

The Nasty Nibbles

"No man is free who cannot command himself."
                                                        Pythagoras

There is a darling friend of mine who has had a weight problem ever since I've known her. We've talked a lot about it, and this year she really made the commitment to lose the weight and keep it off.

"I love the Lord," she said, "but I can see it all now. I have told Him I want to obey His commandments. I will spend my whole life going to church, not missing my meetings, not drinking coffee, liquor, or tea, nor smoking. I will pay my tithes and offerings, be charitable, visit the sick and needy. Yes, I can see it all now. After I've put in a hard life's work and I get to the pearly gates, the gatekeeper will tell me I can't come in because I'm still thirty pounds overweight."

"If I'm going to blow it," she continued, "I want to blow it for something really big, not thirty pounds!"

Of course, she said all this in humor, but she was serious, too. She knew that if she could have the self-discipline to do all the Lord asked, she would have to be master of her own body, perhaps her greatest responsibility.

I also love the friend who told me about her first pregnancy. She is a 33-year-old wife and mother of three children and always arrives looking like an 8" × 10" glossy. With her first baby, she gained seventy-four pounds! My face echoed shock, and I expressed disbelief as I gazed upon this size three individual.

"Listen, Honey," she said, "I would have gained a lot more, but I only had two hands!"

There is another woman I know who also had had a weight problem all her life. She is much older than I am, and her children are all away from home. She is also very close to being six feet tall. When we first met about ten years ago, she impressed me as an energetic, vivacious, on-the-go woman. That impression has never faded. She is a wonderful woman to be around, full of life. Ten years ago she defended her weight and size vigorously. She would always say, "I am big. I was born big. Big is beautiful. I'll always be a big woman." She always dressed most attractively. Once I remember seeing her in a dress that looked like a big, black tent with a red rose at the neck. She was trying to *cover it all up,* but she was also making a definite statement that she cared about what she looked like.

A few years ago she went on a strict diet and lost over fifty pounds. She looks sensational! The weight loss has changed her life. She once wore a heavy hairstyle, thinking it helped hide the fat and offset her height. Now she wears a short, stylish cut that flatters her eyes and face. She also didn't wear make-up because she thought it attracted too much attention to the fat lines on her face. Now she wears light make-up that gives her color and warmth. Her clothes were clean and attractive but always of the tent variety. Now her wardrobe is tailored and trim and, for the first time in her life, full of skirts, blouses, and even belts!

She told me that not only did she look years younger, she felt years younger. And despite her nearly six-foot frame, she feels feminine and lovely for the first time since she has been married. Her husband even took her on a second honeymoon!

I became acquainted with S. Scott Zimmerman, Ph.D., a professor of biochemistry at Brigham Young University, after reading an article he had written for the *Ensign Magazine.* His article was based on data that showed obesity to be a biochemical problem. I was intrigued. He also discussed exercise, specifically endurance exercise, as a program to lose weight and control obesity. I was excited! There had been many things which I had read on the subject of endurance exercise which definitely showed great progress in the war against obesity. There was more — I felt S. Scott Zimmerman's great spirit! His attitude was positive and uplifting. I felt impressed to contact him immediately. He enlightened me even more regarding his subject, and we found we shared the same POSITIVE attitude and ideas about weight control and exercise.

The following article is presented with his permission. It represents some of the findings of his research, as well as some of his ideas concerning weight control.

Fitness and Nutrition
by
Dr. S. Scott Zimmerman

Losing weight is a national pastime. Millions of Americans have lost many millions of pounds of body fat. Books on dieting are national best sellers. Weekly newspapers at the grocery store checkout counters boast of new, fail-proof diets. There are low carbohydrate diets, high protein diets, high fiber diets, grapefruit and egg diets, exotic herb diets, starvation diets, and even eat-all-you-want diets. Magazine ads push various products to help "melt away ugly fat." There are vibrators and rollers and body slinkies and steamers and a plethora of other gadgets for sure-fire weight reduction. Drugs and medication are promoted as cures for obesity. And Americans run from one fad to the next in search of the secret to convert their bodies from an Erma Bombeck to a Cheryl Tiegs.

But gaining — or I should say re-gaining — weight is an even more popular American pastime. Two of the hottest businesses of the late 1970s were fitness spas and fast-food joints. As Americans, we are good at taking it off, but even better at putting it back on. Over 90 percent of those who go on a diet fail to lose weight or they regain whatever weight they lost. And in spite of our superabundance of diets and weight-loss gadgets and medications and health spas and fitness clinics, over 50 percent of the adults in America are still overweight. Among women in the United States, the problem is even worse: over 60 percent are overweight.

Why do diets fail? Before answering this, let's examine why people are overweight in the first place.

Why Obesity?

Your answer, and almost everyone's answer to the question of why people are overweight, is that they eat too much. This is only partially true. Obviously you can't gain weight from food you don't eat. But the answer is an over-simplification. Much research published in the scientific literature has revealed that the answer is much more complex. Let me cite several research findings which indicate that obesity is not just a simple problem of lack of self-discipline in eating.

1. Obese people *don't* eat more than those around them of normal weight. Research has shown that some people will gain weight on the same diet on which others will remain trim.
2. Several studies have shown that diets of obese children are not significantly different from diets of normal children. The reason for the excess fat lies beyond the simple matter of too much food intake.
3. Research has shown that, while the average weight of Americans is on the rise, the per capita caloric intake is decreasing.
4. Volunteer subjects from slimming clubs were incarcerated and observed for three weeks. Fed a 1,500-calorie-per-day diet (which in theory should yield a two-pound-per-week weight loss), nineteen individuals lost weight, nine maintained their weight, and two actually gained weight.
5. In another study, a group of subjects were persuaded to eat 7,000 to 10,000

calories per day for 200 days or more, with an expected weight increase of twenty to twenty-five percent. Some reached the expected weight with ease, but others did so only with much difficulty, and others failed to gain any weight at all even though they consumed more than those who gained readily.

6. Certain hormones and other body chemicals have been discovered recently which are involved in the hunger response. Hunger is a complex physiological and psychological phenomenon probably involving the release of "hunger" hormones. The conditions under which these hormones are released are not fully understood, but it is possible that in some people their release is not properly controlled.

7. Research has suggested that being overweight is in part hereditary. For example, children separated from their parents at an early age have a greater chance of being like their natural parents than their adopted parents in terms of degree of obesity. It is also known that if one of your parents is overweight, you have a 50 percent chance of becoming overweight, and if both parents are overweight, your chances increase to 80 percent.

The Diet Cycle

The conclusion I come to — and many scientists have also come to — is that weight control diets are not the total answer in solving weight problems. To better understand this, let me give you what I call the Diet Cycle. This is what happens when a typical Mormon woman, Jane Doe, goes on a diet.

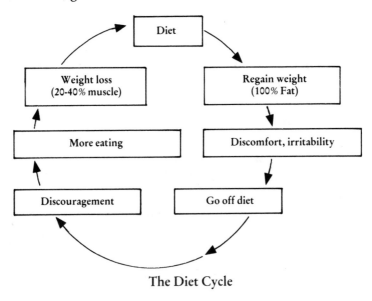

The Diet Cycle

FIRST, Jane Doe stands in front of a mirror, sees rolls of ugly fat, and decides to go on a diet. Almost invariably the diet involves limiting caloric intake, so Jane starts eating less.

SECOND, Jane loses some weight. Weight loss is what she wanted, and weight loss is what she got. However, unbeknown to Jane, twenty to forty percent of her weight loss was muscle — not ugly excess fat but beautiful much-needed muscle protein. Let's assume Jane lost ten pounds. That means she lost about six pounds of fat, which is good, and four pounds of muscle, which is bad.

Obviously Jane's body resists the idea that needed protein is being burned as fuel, so THIRD in the Diet Cycle, Jane feels discomfort and irritability. If you have lived with or personally been a dieter, you know the general malaise of a starving person. As everyone who's tried it knows, going on a diet is no fun. Jane is miserable. Her husband and children are miserable.

FOURTH, Janes goes off her diet. This is almost inevitable. The psychological and physiological discomfort of having her muscle protein waste away drains Jane of her desire to stay on her diet. The miserable means (dieting) does not justify the hoped for end (slimness).

FIFTH, now Jane is discouraged. She had set a goal to lose twenty pounds, she lost only ten, and she's off her diet. Since she knows nothing about the physiology of weight loss and nothing about the research showing that her diet was a bad idea in the first place, she feels she lacks self-discipline. Her self-image, strained in the first place by her weight problem, now dips to a new low.

SIXTH, if Jane is like most overweight people, her discouragement leads to more eating or even to "binge" eating.

SEVENTH, Jane regains the ten pounds she lost.

That completes the cycle. Jane is now ready to go on another diet, and the cycle repeats itself. The famous nutritionist, Dr. Jean Mayer, calls this the "rhythm method of girth control."

If going through the cycle was a simple matter of a failed diet, things wouldn't be so bad. But things are not the same as they were before Jane went on her diet. True, she is now the same weight as she was, but she is actually fatter because a greater percent of her body weight is fat. Recall, Jane lost ten pounds and regained ten pounds, but only six of the lost pounds were fat, the rest were muscle; however, all of the ten pounds regained are fat! So Jane's diet has made her four pounds fatter, that is, she has a higher percent body fat even though she is the same weight.

And that's not Jane's only problem. Besides now carrying more fat, she has less muscle tissue. Since muscle tissue burns calories but fat tissue doesn't, Jane now must eat less to maintain the same weight! In other words if, after regaining the weight lost on her diet, Jane eats the same as she did before the diet, she will gain even more weight.

We can draw a surprising but true conclusion from Jane Doe's diet experience: Dieting makes people fatter!

So what is the answer? How can Jane Doe break out of this diet cycle? Unfortunately, there is no magic formula nor secret potion nor miracle gadget. There is, however, a well-documented solution to Jane's weight problem:

Exercise.

Much research by many scientists of divergent backgrounds and disciplines has shown that obesity can be overcome and controlled through the right kind of exercise coupled with proper diet. I stress "the right kind" of exercise because many people jog a mile a day or play tennis three times a week and see no effect on body weight. The right kind of exercise is an *endurance* exercise, involving the large lower-body muscle groups, is repetitive in nature, and is carried out for an extended period of time at a relatively slow pace. Examples include walking, jogging, bicycling, swimming, hiking, and aerobic dancing. How long and how slow will be discussed later. The important thing to understand is that the cause of obesity — genetic problems, enzyme deficiencies, hormone imbalances, and other problems mentioned earlier — are usually overcome through endurance exercise.

The Endurance Exercise Cycle

Now let's return to Jane Doe, standing in front of her bedroom mirror, deciding that something must be done about her midriff flab. But now Jane decides that, rather than go on a diet, she will begin an endurance exercise program. Instead of getting caught in the Diet Cycle, she begins what I call the Endurance Exercise Cycle. It goes like this (see page 37):

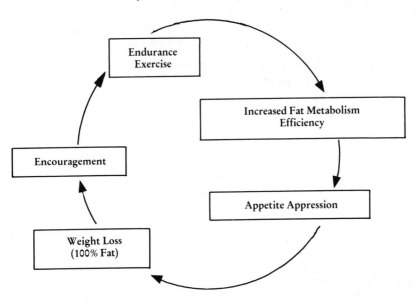

Endurance Exercise

Increased Fat Metabolism Efficiency

Encouragement

Appetite Appression

Weight Loss (100% Fat)

The Endurance Exercise Cycle

FIRST, Jane starts to exercise. Exactly how and what she does will be considered later.

SECOND, her efficiency at burning fat begins to increase. If Jane is out of shape and overweight, she probably has a very inefficient fat-burning system. She probably has plenty of well-used enzymes for storing fat but is deficient in those for breaking down fat. Endurance exercise promotes fat-burning efficiency.

THIRD, Jane notices a relative decrease in her appetite. Most of us think exercise stimulates the appetite. This is probably true for short, fast exercise sessions, but this is not true for endurance exercise relative to the number of calories burned. Research has shown that most people will respond to endurance exercise with a decrease in appetite so that the desire to eat back the calories burned through exercise is suppressed.

FOURTH, Jane loses fat. Sometimes the actual weight stays the same, because muscle tissue is being made in response to the exercise, but inevitably there is fat loss and usually total weight loss as well.

FIFTH, Jane is encouraged in her weight loss. She does not feel the discomfort of degrading her body protein because she is actually increasing in muscle protein. She is not irritable from starving herself because she hasn't had to starve herself. And she feels better about herself because she is more physically fit and physically stronger. Exercise provides a psychological and emotional lift as well as physical benefit.

That completes one turn of the Endurance Exercise Cycle. And then the cycle starts again. Because Jane feels good and is encouraged by her weight loss, she remains physically active, or becomes more active, which further increases her fat-burning efficiency, and so on.

An Endurance Exercise Program

I would now like to present a simple endurance exercise program which can be used by most people. Some people, especially those who are very heavy, have been physically inactive for some time, are advanced in years, or have some other health problem, should consult a physician before embarking on any exercise program. The following plan is designed for an average person, 18-50 years old, of average fitness, in relatively good health (except for being over-weight).

1. *Walk ten miles per week spread over four or more days.* I suggest you start out trying to walk one mile. If you begin to feel weary during the walk, slow down or stop. The key here is to start easy, go slow, and not overdo. Make your exercise enjoyable. In a proper endurance exercise plan, there is no place for pain (although maybe a *little* discomfort). If your first mile goes well, try going farther the next day. Continue to walk only — no running — until you can cover about two miles a day, five days a week. That is, gradually increase your distance to ten miles of walking per week, spread over at least four days during the week. Some people starting out can walk the full ten miles per week; others will require a few weeks to move up to that distance. After doing ten miles per week of just walking, if you would like, gradually start to mix in a little slow jogging. For example, in your two-mile exercise, you might try to slowly run a block, walk two to three blocks, run a block, walk two to three blocks, and so on. If the running becomes painful or unduly fatiguing or especially

39

if it induces dizziness, return to walking, or stop altogether. The biggest problem in a fitness program is not lack of determination but too much of it; overdoing can precipitate stress injuries, soreness, undue tiredness, or even heart problems. Use your determination to patiently keep at the program, not to walk or run more than your body can handle.

Gradually increase the amount of walking (or slow jogging) until you are covering all ten miles per week. Now you are ready to go to the next step.

2. *Increase your weekly distance to twenty miles.* The increase should be gradual. Never walk (or run) more than two miles farther in one week than you did the week before. Never increase mileage from one week to the next if you experience undue stress or fatigue. Have the courage to hold back. Your muscles, tendons, and ligaments take time to adjust to the stress of long distance walking.

    Twenty miles per week is your goal. Although jogging will provide a little more benefit than walking, don't jog unless you want to. Similarly, brisk walking will provide more benefit than slow walking, so move briskly, but keep it enjoyable.

3. *Eat a balanced diet.* Don't worry so much about food as you did while on a weight

reduction diet, but certainly don't over-eat. The main focus of this program is the exercise. If, once you are well into the exercise plan, say after six weeks, you want to lose weight a little faster, go ahead and think more about cutting down on your food intake. You probably already will have cut down some naturally. But the main thing is to eat a balanced diet. Just remember the four food groups you learned in grade school: (a) the fruit and vegetable group, (b) the bread and grain group, (c) the meat group (which includes dried beans and nuts), and (d) the dairy group. Eat a good mix of these foods every day.

4. *Listen to your body.* Most people with weight problems have come to think of their bodies as their enemy, anxious to deceive them into ill-health and flabbiness. This is faulty thinking. If you will listen to your body, you will have success in your exercise and in your diet. When you are out walking and your body says something is wrong, stop! When you are sitting at the dinner table and your body starts to feel full, stop eating! When your body feels it needs more sleep, get more sleep! When your body starts to crave more fruits and vegetables and less meat, which invariably happens when you exercise extensively, eat more fruits and vegetables! If you will listen carefully,

your body will help you in getting back to full fitness and health.

That's the plan: (1) walk (and/or run) ten miles per week, (2) up the distance to twenty miles per week, (3) eat a balanced diet, and (4) listen to your body.

Why Walking (or Running)?

In the fitness program just outlined, I suggested walking or running as the main type of exercise. While other types of endurance exercise are just as valuable, and even may be better for you in your particular circumstances, I suggest walking or running because:

1. It is the right kind of exercise. This means it is a repetitive exercise, utilizing the lower-body muscle groups. This feature, of course, is shared by other activities — swimming, cycling, cross-country skiing, etc. — which are also excellent forms of exercise.

2. It is convenient. This is probably the best feature of walking and running. You can do it anytime — early morning, during the day, or late at night — with or without a partner, in any kind of weather, and in any location — around a track, across fields, on roads and sidewalks, along the beach, through city parks, or along mountain paths.

3. It is inexpensive. Your only expense is a good pair of running shoes, at a cost of $25-$40. True, you can spend a lot on

jogging outfits, but they are unnecessary.

4. It is fun. You probably don't believe me since your only running before this has been one-mile jogs or laps around the practice field as part of your high school P.E. class. But just take my word for it. Once you get up to twenty miles per week, you will be physically fit, probably for the first time in your life, and your walks and runs will be pain-free adventures. Exercising with your spouse or children or friends is fun. Walking to see nature — the mountains, the fields, the sky, the flowers — is fun. Walking for prayer and meditation has been beneficial and enjoyable to many. Just remember, almost everyone finds exercise uncomfortable and boring until they get up to about twenty miles per week. After that — well, get into shape and find out for yourself how enjoyable it can be.

Why Twenty Miles Per Week?

A common question is, "Why twenty miles per week? Why can't I get by on five or ten a week?" Let me give you four main reasons:

1. To reduce weight and control body fat. At ten miles of walking per week, the fat-burning efficiency in most people is still not developed well enough for significant weight loss. But twenty miles a week will handle even the most stubborn fat. Moreover, running twenty miles a week

burns over 2,000 calories, or about two-thirds of a pound of fat. In terms of food, it is the equivalent of two big meals. Walking twenty miles a week will burn about 1,800 calories, which amounts to a weight loss of almost thirty pounds a year. So for losing weight, walking twenty miles is quite significant. Walking or running twenty miles a week also stimulates a significant increase in body muscle mass, thus not only making you stronger, but also increasing your basal metabolic rate, that is, the amount of calories you burn while just sitting around. This means you can eat the same and lose weight.

2. To increase cardiovascular fitness and decrease the risk of heart attack. Although heart attack once was considered a disease primarily afflicting men, increasing numbers of women are becoming victims. There is considerable evidence that jogging a mile a day or playing tennis three days a week has no significant effect on reducing the risk of cardiovascular disease. But several recently published research reports show that the risk of cardiovascular disease *is* significantly reduced by exercising at the level of 1,800 to 2,000 calories per week. As stated before, running twenty miles burns about 2,000 calories and walking that distance burns 1,800 calories.

3. To overcome "type A" behavior. One of the suspected causes of cardiovascular disease is the so-called "type A" behavior. Type A people are those who are aggressive, are driven by internal and external pressures, and are slaves to the clock (constantly trying to do things faster and get more done in a shorter period of time). Long, slow walking and running are the antitheses of type A behavior. They are gentle, noncompetitive, and nonaggressive. They allow you to get out-of-doors, to get away from the pressures of life, and to be alone. Or they allow leisurely conversation with friends and family or relaxed sight-seeing of your neighborhood. This is in contrast to mile-a-day jogging or thrice-a-week tennis playing, which often promotes competition and aggression and becomes one more item for the type A personality to do "faster" and "better" and "more efficiently."
4. To make exercise enjoyable. It's a case of more being easier. At about twenty miles per week, you become free of discomfort and boredom.

Diet and Nutrition

Although I have stressed the importance of exercise in developing cardiovascular fitness and in controlling weight, I do not want to minimize the importance of proper nutrition and diet. The most effective program for developing a healthy body is by a combination of prudent diet and regular endurance exercise.

A prudent diet involves a balance of the four food groups mentioned earlier. Let's review them one at a time:

1. *The Milk Group.* These dairy products provide needed protein, riboflavin (vitamin B_2), and calcium. The recommended daily intake is two servings for adults, four servings for teenagers, and three servings for children. If you are pregnant or lactating, you should have four servings a day. Examples of a serving include one cup of milk, yogurt or pudding, one and three-fourths cups ice cream, two cups cottage cheese, or one and one-half slices of cheddar cheese. (Each of these is based upon an equivalent amount of calcium.) If you are trying to watch your weight, emphasize skim milk (or 2%) and cottage cheese, and de-emphasize sweetened pudding and ice cream.

2. *The Meat Group.* Meats and related foods are rich in protein, niacin (a B vitamin), thiamin (vitamin B_1), and iron. In America, the importance of meat has been blown way out of proportion, and ironically this is true even among Mormons. The Doctrine and Covenants specifically states that flesh of beasts and fowl "are to be used sparingly." This is in harmony

with much scientific research on the ill effects of excess meat, particularly red meats (beef, ham, and the like). The recommended intake is two small servings per day, three if you are pregnant. Exercise does *not* increase the demand for protein. One serving includes only two ounces of cooked, lean meat, fish, or poultry, or two eggs, two (2 oz.) slices of cheddar cheese (not to be used for both meat and milk groups), one cup dried beans or peas, or four tablespoons of peanut butter. (Cheer up, Mothers! You don't have to feel guilty giving your kids peanut butter sandwiches.) It is wise to keep in mind that foods of the meat group do not have to be meat, that red meats are high in calories and cholesterol, and that 70 percent of the calories in hamburger is from fat.

Now I have warned of the potential problems of meats (high cholesterol and high calories), I should warn women of the potential danger of neglecting the meat group. Women in their childbearing years are very susceptible to iron deficiency. Iron is a key nutrient in hemoglobin, the oxygen-carrying protein in the blood. Lack of iron can lead to anemia and other diseases. Many experts therefore feel that women should take iron supplements; but this should only be done under the direction of a physician. Proper intake of foods rich in iron should be sufficient. These include liver and kidney, which are the best sources of iron, and also oysters, shrimp, sardines, other meats, dried beans, most nuts, eggs, prunes, raisins, green leafy vegetables, and enriched breads and cereals.

3. *The Fruit-Vegetable Group.* While meat is overemphasized in the American diet, fruits and vegetables are unfortunately neglected. Here again the Doctrine and Covenants gives good advice: "All wholesome herbs hath God ordained for . . . the use of man . . . and every fruit . . . to be used with prudence" (D&C 89:10,11). The dictionary defines herb as a "seed-producing plant that does not develop woody tissue but dies down at the end of a growing season," and defines vegetable as "an herbaceous plant grown for an edible part which is used for food." Fruits and vegetables provide energy in the form of carbohydrates and vitamins A and C. Dark green, leafy, or orange vegetables and fruits are recommended three or four times weekly for vitamin A, and citrus fruits or tomato juice daily for vitamin C. In general you should have four servings per day (regardless of age, pregnancy, or lactation). A typical serving is one-half cup cooked vegetable or juice, one cup raw vegetable, or one

medium-sized apple or banana. In "Dietary Goals for the United States," second edition (1977), prepared by the Select Committee on Nutrition and Human Needs of the United States Senate, some of the major goals are to "increase the consumption of complex carbohydrates and 'naturally occurring' sugars" and "decrease overall fat consumption" and "decrease cholesterol consumption." In practical terms this means increasing intake of fruits and vegetables and decreasing intake of fatty food and red meats.

4. *The Grain Group.* Again Section 89 provides excellent guidelines: "All grain is ordained for the use of man" (v. 14). The Senate Select Committee on Nutrition, 114 years later, supports this suggestion: "Increase consumption . . . of whole grains." The recommended consumption for all people is four helpings per day. A typical helping is one slice of bread, or one cup ready-to-eat cereal, or one-half cup cooked cereal, pasta, or grits. Grains are a good source of carbohydrates, thiamin, iron, and niacin.

Although this seems like a lot to worry about, it can be simplified by the summary statement, "eat a little bit of a lot of different things." This is good advice whether you are trying to lose weight or not.

Exercise and Women

There are several recurring questions asked by women who have attended one of my classes or firesides on fitness and weight control or who have read my article "Running Away from It All: A Guide to Fitness and Weight Control" (*Ensign*, February, 1981). Here are some of the questions and my answers:

Should women follow the same exercise program as men? The ultimate goal of twenty miles of walking or running per week is the same for men and women, but usually women take a little longer reaching the goal, and often (but definitely not always) cover the distance slower than most men. This is only because men usually have a history of more exercise and therefore are in better shape when they start. The main principle to keep in mind is that you should start at your own level and progress at your own pace, not the ones set by your neighbor or your husband. It's great to exercise with your husband, but let him know that he will have to go at your pace (going slower will do him just as much good as going faster, and going faster will not be good for you).

I feel embarrassed about exercising in public, especially since I am overweight. What should I do? Here are several suggestions: (1) exercise in the early morning before your neighbors wake up; (2) use an exercycle (stationary bicycle — make sure you buy a high quality exercycle, as a cheap one will discourage exercise, and you will be tempted to give it up); (3) exercise with a group of other women — disdain from sedentary neighbors is easier to take if you have company; (4) walk to the grocery store and back and tell people you are doing it to save gas (not a bad idea in its own right!); and (5) don't worry about what others think. (Your health and weight control are more important than their shallow thinking.) Actually, exercise is so popular nowadays that very few people will give your exercise a second thought.

How should I run, toe or heel first? One problem women have is a desire to look feminine while walking or running, and so they exercise too daintily. Just be natural. This is always heel before toe in walking and should be the same in running. Another problem women have is the tendency to hold their arms too high. When you jog, your forearms should be about waist high and parallel to the ground.

Do I need a special bra? Running stores sell special running bras, but many world-class runners wear no bra at all and have no difficulty. Just make sure you get enough support that you are not self-conscious of any possible bouncing.

Won't running cause drooping breasts? No. Running will in fact strengthen the pectoral muscles to give you more support.

Won't running give me big, bulky muscles? Walking and running will strenghten muscles and increase (to a certain degree) the total muscle mass. But endurance exercise will lead to long, slender muscles, not short stubby ones. Just think of the Olympic women gymnasts, some of the strongest and most physically fit women in the world. They have slender, lithe, beautiful bodies!

What should I do about muggers, rapists, and hecklers? First of all don't worry about muggers, since potential robbers can plainly see that you aren't carrying your purse. Hecklers are usually harmless, although annoying. Just ignore them. Rape is a problem worth thinking about. Most of these problems can be solved by exercising during daylight, with other women or family members (even a small child), and in open areas. Obviously you should avoid frequent walks or runs alone along secluded paths. If you have to exercise at night or before sunup, do so in a well-lit area and with other people. If you live in or near a rough neighborhood, you might want to use an exercycle or go to a public swimming pool or a school track for your exercise. Many large cities have public jogging paths in parks, which have now become safe because of the large number of people who jog there.

How should I handle an aggressive dog? Most dogs are only interested in defending their territory, so a first solution is simply to move to the other side of the street. If a dog looks like he might try to chase you, stop, face the dog, reach down for a rock (or *act* like you are reaching for a rock), throw or feign throwing the rock, then back away slowly and continue your walk. You also may want to carry a stick.

My husband is always nagging me to lose weight. What should I do? Have him read this:

"Husbands, nagging your wife about her weight will only make things worse. Control your words and your feelings and accept your wife the way she is. If you are really serious about wanting your wife to lose weight, help her follow the suggestions in this chapter. Tell her, 'Dear, you go out and walk for an hour while I finish supper and take care of the kids!' "

Should I exercise when I feel depressed? Mild depression is very common among women, and Mormon women are not immune. The pressures of home, children, and church responsibilities can cause depression in even the most emotionally stable women. Considerable experience and research by psychologists and psychiatrists have shown exercise to be an effective antidote for depression. In fact, seriously depressed men and women use exercise to effectively replace drugs in their therapy. A study, by nutritionists and exercise physiologists at Brigham Young University, of the effects of exercise on overweight women reported that the psychological and emotional benefits, as reported by the women subjects, were as impressive as the physical benefits.

Will exercise help other physical and emotional problems? Studies have shown that endurance exercise can be effective in treating chronic headaches, constipation, insomnia, and other ailments common to our modern way of life. If you have serious problems, consult a physician before embarking on an exercise program, since some problems are accentuated by exercise.

Should I exercise during menstruation? Some women cut down or stop exercise during their period because of the discomfort of cramps. Others feel exercise alleviates cramps. Do some experimenting on your own. There is certainly no physiological or medical problem with exercising during menstruation. There is even some report that exercise helps alleviate dysmenorrhea (painful or difficult menstruation).

Should older women whose bones are weak exercise? Consult your physician on this matter. However, mild exercise should be safe for most healthy older women. I might add, research suggests that some forms of arthritis and idiopathic osteoporosis (a common, post-menopause bone disease) can be partially alleviated by endurance exercise. The best advice is to stay active while young so that the problems usually associated with old age will be forestalled.

Answers to Other Common Questions

Will your exercise-weight control program work for everyone? I wish I could give an unqualified yes. It is definitely true that if you are now eating just enough to maintain your weight, don't increase your food intake, and start to exercise, you will lose weight. The laws of conservation of mass and energy demand it. It is equally true that even without exercise, you will lose weight if you eat less. But there is a catch: dieting is painful, and most people can't endure a lifetime of pain. My experience is that the right kind of exercise is so much less painful than dieting, eventually becomes enjoyable, and has so many benefits besides losing weight, that many people lose weight through exercise (and proper nutrition) where dieting alone failed before. But many people give up on an exercise program before they get to the point where it does them good and before it becomes enjoyable.

Do you know many people who have lost weight through exercise? Yes, many people. I personally went from 210 to 165 pounds. I know many other men and women who have lost 25 to 80 pounds through exercise, and *the very best part is they are keeping it off.*

How fast will I lose the weight? People spend years getting 25, 30, 50 or more pounds overweight and then want to take it all off in three weeks. Patience is the great virtue for weight loss and fitness. Your first concern should be to *slowly* build up your exercise program to 20 miles per week, while you maintain or moderately cut down on your food consumption. You will burn off fat by doing this. But let me warn you. Many people don't lose a lot of weight immediately because the exercise increases their muscle weight while they are taking off fat. Initially a better way to determine your progress is by measuring your waistline. But eventually you'll lose pounds also. It is a highly individual matter, dependent upon individual physiological characteristics. For your own health, however, you should not lose faster than two pounds per week.

What if I can't exercise? I don't know the answer to weight loss for those who just can't exercise. My best advice is to eat nutritionally good food and moderately cut down on amounts. Actually very few people are unable to exercise. Swimming, for example, is good for people with rheumatism, bad backs, weak knees, or other structural ailments. Again, if you have questions, consult your physician.

What if I don't need to loss weight? After giving a lecture or fireside on exercise, invariably one or two people approach me afterwards and ask this question. About 80 percent of those people actually could stand to lose a few pounds of fat. Many women who look slim and healthy have kept off pounds through constant dieting, but because they never exercise are actually unfit and need to replace fat tissue with muscle tissue. Everyone needs exercise. So I suggest the same program for everyone: get on a good endurance exercise program. Even if you are underweight, exercise will help you be stronger and look healthier.

Your emphasis on exercise sounds as if you think calories don't count. Is that true? Calories *do* count. The laws of conservation of mass and energy are never violated. Some scientists believe that certain slender individuals have "brown fat," which can burn off calories (to provide heat) and therefore do not gain weight when they eat excessively, but even if this is true, most of us are not so blessed. There is a wide variance in how people handle calories, in how caloric intake affects their appetite, and in how they are able to maintain (or not maintain) their weight, some of which is genetic, and most of which is poorly understood. For those of us with weight problems, counting calories may be very helpful.

I would rather play tennis than walk or jog. Can I get fit playing my favorite sport? No. Although such sports as tennis and racquetball are great to supplement your endurance exercise program, they are not the kind of activities which will provide sufficient cardiovascular fitness and lead to weight control.

But walking or jogging is so boring! This is a common complaint and one I voiced often before I started the *right kind* of exercise program. With slow, endurance exercise, at a high enough level (20 miles per week), to really get into shape, boredom evaporates! If looking at mountains, flowers, farm lands, and neighborhood gardens is boring — if meditating and praying is boring — if talking with friends is boring — then you have a deeper problem than just lack of fitness! I will admit, however, that during the build-up phase exercise may at times be boring.

But I still would rather do other things than walk or jog. What else can I do? Any activity which involves the leg muscles, is repetitive, and can be done for a relatively long period of time at a moderate intensity will provide the kind of fitness you want. If you prefer, you could jump rope, jump on a mini-trampoline, ride an exercycle, cross-country ski, golf (if you walk), aerobic dance, or water jog.

How much do I need of these? Here's a good rule: exercise for 40 minutes per day, five days a week, at an intensity such that your heart rate stays at about 70 percent of its maximum. Your maximum heart rate is approximately 220 minus your age. So if you are 40 years old, your maximum heart rate is 220 − 40 = 180, and 70 percent of that is 126. But also use the "talk test." The activity should never be so intense that you can't talk to someone else while exercising. A word of caution: it takes time to build up to the 40 minutes per day. Start at five to ten minutes and work up slowly from there.

I have heard that fifteen minutes per day is enough. Why do you say forty minutes? Research has shown that the *absolute minimum* amount of exercise to produce any training effect on the heart is fifteen minutes. But I am talking about getting in top cardiovascular fitness and controlling weight. You simply have to put in the extra time to get the extra benefit. Minimal exercise yields minimal results.

Will exercising beyond the twenty miles per week do me more good? Yes — up to a point. The more you exercise, the more calories you burn, and the more fit you become. So I wouldn't discourage (and would encourage in some cases) walking or jogging up to one hour or maybe one and a half hours a day. However, beyond 40-60 minutes, you get rapidly diminishing returns on your time investment, and you also run the risk of stress injuries.

I just don't have the time to exercise. Any suggestions? I don't really believe you lose time by taking out an hour a day for exercise. You will feel better, sleep better, and accomplish more. In addition, many people are able to accomplish other things while walking or jogging — plan their day, prepare talks and lessons in their head, etc. These things are hard to do while you are building your fitness, but once you get to twenty miles a week, you will be able to think about more than "When do I get to stop?" One of the greatest needs of Mormon women is to take time to "smell the roses." You need that hour of exercise to get out of the house, clear your head, and return refreshed and invigorated.

When should I exercise? It makes little difference. For most people, early mornings are convenient because there are fewer conflicts. In my neighborhood, a group of women meet every morning at 6:30 a.m. for their daily walk. For weight loss, I feel the best time is just before supper. Most overeating takes place in the evening, and the workout will help suppress the appetite. But few women have the freedom to leave the house when husband and children are demanding supper.

Do I need special equipment? If you run, a pair of good running shoes is an absolute necessity. A good shoe cushions and stabilizes the foot and helps you avoid stress injuries (shin splints, stress fractures, "runner's knee," etc.). Buy shoes from a running store or a sporting goods store and ask for a "Five Star" shoe (rated by *Runner's World*). This will assure you of getting a good shoe at a reasonable price ($30-$50). If you walk, it's also a good idea to get a good running shoe, but the requirement isn't as important.

Is running a lot better than walking? If you run a mile (depending upon your weight), you burn about 100-130 calories. If you walk a mile (depending upon your weight *and* your pace), you burn about 80-100 calories. So actually twenty miles of running is the equivalent of twenty-five miles of walking. But I don't quibble over five miles per week.

Doesn't running faster do more good? No. If you cover the same distance, almost regardless of how fast you run or jog you will burn the same number of calories. If you go slower, it will just take you longer. This is why I prefer to suggest exercise *distances* rather than exercise *times.* Of course, if you run for forty minutes, you will burn many more calories than if you walk for forty minutes, and hence the training effect will be better. However, running faster than the "talk test" rate (see above) will *not* be better than running slowly. So slow down and enjoy your exercise!

Should I eat more protein and salt once I start exercising? An emphatic no! Just eat according to the guidelines given above. You will want to drink water before, during (if possible), and after exercise. It's an old wives' tale that water and exercise will cause cramps.

I want to lose weight just around my midriff. How can I do this? Unfortunately you can't tell your body where it will lose its fat. You can firm up your abdomen by sit-ups and other calisthenics, but the only way to lose fat from any particular place is to lose it from all over through endurance exercise and diet.

Will I live longer with exercise and proper diet? Although this has not been conclusively proven scientifically, there is a tremendous body of indirect, scientific evidence suggesting you will live longer. More important however, than quantity is quality of life. Those who obey the rules of good health will have "health in their navel and marrow to their bones; and shall find wisdom and great treasures of knowledge, . . . and shall run and not be weary, and shall walk and not faint. And I, the Lord, give unto them a promise, that the destroying angel shall pass by them." (D&C 89:18-21.)

Further Reading

Jean Mayer. *A Diet for Living.* New York: Simon & Schuster Pocket Books, 1975.

Select Committee on Nutrition and Human Needs, U. S. Senate. *Dietary Goals for the United States.* Second edition. Washington: U. S. Government Printing Office, 1977. (Order from the Superintendent of Documents, U. S. Government Printing Office, Washington, D.C. 20402, Stock no. 052-070-04376-8.)

Garth Fisher and Robert Conlee. *The Complete*

Book of Physical Fitness. Provo: BYU Press, 1979.

James F. Fixx. *The Complete Book of Running.* New York: Random House, 1977.

Calories DO count, as Dr. Zimmerman has stated. The following diet plans are ones used by my gynecologist, a prominent and well-respected doctor in Nevada, O. H. Christofferson, M.D. They have been devised by medical researchers and dieticians for the Carnation Company and are based on the four basic food groups. A basic meal plan is outlined and a sample menu given. A list of foods to substitute and interchange on the sample menu is also included along with a diet plan for pregnancy and lactation.

The diet plan for reducing is based on 1,200 calories per day, and the side columns tell what to do if you want to lower it to 1,000 calories or increase it to 1,500 per day.

If you want to calculate how many calories you need to cut down to per day, use this formula: An average person doing an average amount of work per day requires fifteen calories per pound of body weight per day to maintain their present body weight.

If you weigh 150 pounds: 150 × 15 calories = 2,250 calories per day.

If you want to lose weight and weigh less than 150 pounds, you must eat less than 2,250 calories per day. To determine how many less, use this formula: There are 3,500 calories stored in each pound of body fat. To lose one pound, you must eat 3,500 calories *less* than you normally eat. So, if you eat 500 less calories per day, you should have a deficit of 3,500 calories in seven days and therefore lose one pound.

Remember, these are theoretical. Dr. Zimmerman pointed out the irregularity of calorie counting. However, when combined with endurance exercise, you have a solid chance at weight loss and control.

How much should you weigh? Here is a chart used by the medical profession to help you determine your ideal weight.

	HEIGHT (WITH SHOES ON) 1-INCH HEELS		SMALL FRAME	MEDIUM FRAME	LARGE FRAME
	Feet	Inches			
M	5	2	112-120	119-119	126-141
E	5	3	115-123	121-133	129-144
N	5	4	118-126	124-136	132-148
	5	5	121-129	127-139	135-152
	5	6	124-133	130-143	138-156
	5	7	128-137	134-147	142-161
	5	8	132-141	138-152	147-166
	5	9	136-145	142-156	151-170
	5	10	140-150	146-160	155-174
	5	11	144-154	150-165	159-179
	6	0	148-158	154-170	164-181
	6	1	152-162	158-175	168-189
	6	2	156-167	162-180	173-191
	6	3	160-171	167-185	178-199
	6	4	164-175	172-190	182-204

	HEIGHT (WITH SHOES ON) 2-INCH HEELS		SMALL FRAME	MEDIUM FRAME	LARGE FRAME
	Feet	Inches			
W	4	10	92- 98	96-107	104-119
O	4	11	94-101	98-110	106-122
M	5	0	96-104	101-113	109-125
E	5	1	99-107	104-116	112-128
N	5	2	102-110	107-119	115-131
	5	3	105-113	110-122	118-134
	5	4	108-116	113-126	121-138
	5	5	111-119	116-130	125-142
	5	6	114-123	120-135	129-146
	5	7	118-127	124-139	133-150
	5	8	122-131	128-143	137-154
	5	9	126-135	132-147	141-158
	5	10	130-140	136-151	145-163
	5	11	134-144	140-155	149-168
	6	0	138-148	141-159	153-173

For girls between 18 and 25, subtract 1 pound for each year under 25.

It isn't just a matter of physical beauty to be the correct weight, it is a matter of your good health. You are subject to fatigue, inefficiency, depression, illness, and any surgery becomes more dangerous when you are overweight. It's your life you should consider.

REDUCING DIET PLAN
1200 Calories Per Day
GENERAL INSTRUCTIONS

The principles of the Reducing Diet Plan are as follows:

Eat regularly — do not omit a meal.

Between meal snacks should be chosen from the free list.

Vary the sample menu by choosing different foods as offered in the indicated substitution lists. Eat those foods in the measured amounts indicated. Noon and evening basic meal plans may be interchanged when desired.

Choose a good source of Vitamin C daily. They are citrus fruits, strawberries, broccoli, brussels sprouts, papaya, and cantaloupe.

Choose a good source of Vitamin A every other day. These are dark green or yellow fruits and vegetables.

Broiling, roasting, steaming, boiling, or baking methods of food preparation are preferable. Avoid the use of fats and oils except in the amounts allowed. Avoid sugar, honey, concentrated sweets, pies, cakes, pastry, rich desserts, regular soft drinks.

Follow a regular exercise program as directed by your physician.

BASIC MEAL PLAN	SAMPLE MENU	SPECIAL INSTRUCTIONS
BREAKFAST 1 serving fruit—List 3 1 measure meat/fish/fowl/ cheese—List 5 1 serving starch—List 4 1 serving fat—List 6 Miscellaneous—List 1 1 serving nonfat milk Miscellaneous—List 1	**BREAKFAST** 1 grapefruit half 1 poached egg 1 slice toast 1 strip bacon Dietetic jelly 1 cup Carnation Instant Nonfat Milk	☐ 1000 Calories; Omit 1 serving nonfat milk, 1 serving starch and 1 serving fat per day from basic meal plan. ☐ 1500 Calories: Add 2 measures meat, 1 serving starch, 1 serving fat, and 1 serving fruit per day to basic meal plan.
NOON MEAL 2 measures meat/fish/fowl/ cheese—List 5 1 serving starch—List 4 1 serving vegetable—List 1 1 serving vegetable—List 2 1 serving fruit—List 3 1 serving nonfat milk	**NOON MEAL** 2 oz. Roast Turkey 3 Ry-Krisp Celery sticks 3 carrot sticks ½ medium apple 1 cup Carnation Instant Nonfat Milk	

BASIC MEAL PLAN	SAMPLE MENU	SPECIAL INSTRUCTIONS

EVENING MEAL
1 serving vegetable—List 1
1 serving fat—List 6
4 measures meat/fish/fowl/
  cheese—List 5
Miscellaneous—List 1
1 serving starch—List 4
1 serving vegetable—List 1
Dessert—List 1
Miscellaneous—List 1
	EVENING MEAL
	Lettuce salad with
	1 Tb. French dressing
	4 oz. Broiled Halibut garnished
	  with chopped parsley &
	  lemon slices
	½ cup steamed rice
	Asparagus spears
	Dietetic gelatin	

BEDTIME 1 serving Slender w/nonfat milk	**BEDTIME** 1 package Carnation Slender with 6 ounces nonfat milk	

SUBSTITUTION LISTS

LIST 1 FREE FOOD LIST: These foods may be used as often as desired provided cream, sugar or honey, or fat is NOT added to them.

Miscellaneous: Clear broth, bouillon, beverages (artificially sweetened containing less than 5 calories per 8 ounces), jelly (artificially sweetened), pickles (dill), parsley, herbs, spices, seasonings, flavorings, vinegar, mustard, horseradish, pickles (sour).

Desserts and Fruits: Cranberries, lemons, gelatin (unsweetened), rennet tablets, rhubarb.

Juices: Lemon juice, tomato juice, vegetable juice.

Vegetables: Asparagus, bean sprouts, beet greens, broccoli, brussels sprouts, cabbage (all kinds), cauliflower, celery, chard, chicory, collard greens, cucumbers, dandelion greens, escarole, eggplant, green beans, kale, lettuce (all kinds), mushrooms, mustard greens, okra, peppers (green or red), radishes, sauerkraut, spinach, squash (summer), tomatoes, turnip greens, watercress, wax beans.

LIST 2 OTHER VEGETABLES: Limit these vegetables to one one-half cup serving per day (approximately 36 calories per serving).

Artichokes, beets, carrots, onions, peas (green), pumpkin, rutabaga, squash (winter), turnips.

LIST 3 FRUITS AND FRUIT JUICES: May be fresh, cooked, dried, frozen, or canned — NO SUGAR OR SYRUP (approximately 40 calories per serving or amounts indicated).

Fruits: Apple, medium — ½; Applesauce — ½ cup; Apricots, medium, fresh — 2; Apricots, dried halves — 4; Banana, small — ½; Blackberries — 1 cup; Blueberries — ⅔ cup; Boysenberries — 1 cup; Cantaloupe, medium — ¼; Cherries, large — 10; Dates — 2; Figs, fresh, large — 1; Figs, dried — 1; Fruit cocktail, canned — ½ cup; Grapefruit, small — ½; Grapes — 12; Honeydew melon — 1/8; Mango, small — ½; Nectarine, small — 1; Orange, small — 1; Papaya, medium — ⅓; Peach, medium, fresh — 1; Peach, canned — ½ cup; Peach, dried halves — 2; Pear, small, fresh — 1; Pear, canned — ½ cup; Pear, dried halves — 2; Pineapple — ½ cup; Plums, medium, fresh — 2; Prunes, dried — 2; Raisins, dried, Tbls. — 2; Raspberries — 1 cup; Strawberries — 1 cup; Tangerine, large — 1; Watermelon, cubed — 1 cup.

Juices: Apple — ⅓ cup; Grape — ¼ cup; Grapefruit — ½ cup; Orange — ½ cup; Pineapple — ⅓ cup; Prune — ¼ cup.

LIST 4 STARCHES: (approximately 68 calories per serving of amounts indicated).

Breads: White, whole wheat, or rye — 1 slice; Bagel — ½; Biscuit or muffin — 1 (2'' diameter); Bun, hamburger or hot dog — ½ (8 to the pound); Cornbread (1½'' cube) — 1; English muffin — ½.

Crackers: Graham (2½'' sq.) — 2; Melba toast — 4; Oyster (½ cup) — 20; Saltine — 5; Round, thin — 6; Ry-Krisp — 3; Tortilla (6'' dia.) — 1.

Cereals: Hot cereal — ½ cup; Dry flakes — ⅔ cup; Dry puffed — 1½ cups; Rice or grits, cooked — ½ cup; Spaghetti, macaroni, noodles, or other pastas, cooked — ½ cup.

Vegetables: Beans or peas, dry cooked (lima, navy, kidney, blackeyed, split, etc.) — ½ cup; Beans, baked (no pork) — ¼ cup; Corn — ⅓ cup or ½ medium ear; Potatoes, white (1 small) — ½ cup; Potatoes, sweet or yams — ¼ cup; Popcorn, popped (no butter) — 1 cup.

LIST 5 MEATS, FISH, FOWL: The following meats and meat substitutes are lowest in calories (approximately 50 calories per amount indicated). Select them as often as possible. Choose lean, unmarbled cuts; trim off all visible fat; do not add fat in cooking.

Beef, dried chipped — 1 oz.; Beef, lamb, pork, ham, veal, LEAN ONLY, cooked — 1 oz.; Liver — 1 oz.; Poultry without skin, cooked — 1 oz.; Fish, any except those listed below — 1 oz.; Crab — ¼ cup; Clams, shrimp, or oysters — 5 medium; Scallops (12/lb.) — 1 large; Tuna, packed in water — ¼ cup; Salmon, pink canned — ¼ cup; Cottage cheese — ¼ cup.

The following meats and meat substitutes are higher in calories (approximately 73 calories per amount indicated). Select them sparingly.

Medium-fat meat (beef, lamb, pork, veal), cooked — 1 oz.; Duck — 1 oz.; Goose — 1 oz.; Poultry with skin — 1 oz.; Cold cuts — 1 oz.; Frankfurters (8-9/lb.) — 1; Vienna sausages — 2; Cheese (brick, cheddar, roquefort, Swiss, processed, etc.) — 1 oz.; Egg, whole — 1; Salmon, red canned or smoked — ¼ cup; Sardines — 3 medium; Tuna, packed in oil — ¼ cup; Peanut butter — 2 Tbls.

LIST 6 FATS (approximately 45 calories per amount indicated).

Avocado (4'' diameter) — 1/8; Bacon, crisp — 1 slice; Butter, margarine — 1 tsp.; Cream, sour — 2 Tbls.; Cream cheese — 1 Tbls.; Nuts — 6 small; Dressing, French — 1 Tbls.; Mayonnaise — 1 tsp.; Roquefort dressing — 2 tsp.; 1000 Island dressing — 2 tsp.; Oil — 1 tsp.; Olives — 5 small.

DIET PLAN DURING PREGNANCY AND LACTATION
GENERAL INSTRUCTIONS

The principles of the pregnancy and lactation diet plan are as follows:

Eat regularly — do not omit a meal.

Choose a minimum of four servings per day from List A, three servings per day from List B, and four servings per day from Lists C & D.

Choose one good source or two fair sources of Vitamin C per day (see List C).

Choose a good source of Vitamin A every other day (see List C).

Follow a regular exercise program as directed by your physician.

Increased nutrient intake is recommended during lactation — add 1 serving from List A per day. Drink two to three quarts fluids per day. The sample menu provides about 1.5 quarts of fluid.

Basic Meal Plan	Sample Menu	Special Instructions
See substituiton list for other allowable foods		Do Not follow the instructions for Sodium Weight Control without your physician's knowledge.
BREAKFAST 1 serving fruit—List C 1 serving meat—List B 1 serving bread—List D 1 serving—List E 1 serving cereal—List D 1 serving—List E 1 serving milk—List A 1 serving—List E	**BREAKFAST** ½ cup orange juice 2 poached eggs 1 slice whole wheat toast with 1 tsp. margarine ¾ cup 40% Bran Flakes with 2 tsp. sugar 1 cup Carnation Instant Nonfat Milk	☐**For Sodium Control** 1. Use salt free margarine and salad dressings. 2. Use salt free bread & cereals only. (Dry cereals contain added salt except for puffed wheat, rice & shredded wheat.) 3. Prepare all foods without salt.
NOON MEAL 1 serving vegetable—List C 1 serving cheese—List B 2 servings bread—List D 2 servings—List E 1 serving vegetable—List C 1 serving fruit—List C 1 serving milk—List A	**NOON MEAL** 7 oz. tomato soup prepared with water 2 oz. Cheddar Cheese on 2 slices white bread, grilled with 2 tsp. margarine ⅔ cup coleslaw 1 medium apple 1 cup Carnation Instant Nonfat Milk	4. Avoid salted or cured meats such as: bacon, sausage, luncheon meats, ham, chipped beef and cheeses. 5. Avoid canned vegetables, canned meats, and meat substitutes unless they are labeled salt-free.

Basic Meal Plan	Sample Menu	Special Instructions

AFTERNOON SNACK
1 serving milk—List A
 	
1 serving—List E
	AFTERNOON SNACK
	1 package Carnation Instant
	  Breakfast made with Carnation
	  Instant Nonfat Milk
	2 Vanilla Wafers
		6. Check with your local water supplier as water may contain a lot of sodium. Distilled water may be necessary

EVENING MEAL
1 serving vegetable—List C
1 serving—List E
2 servings meat—List B
 	
1 serving cereal—List D
1 serving vegetable—List C
1 serving bread/cereal—List D
1 serving—List E
1 serving fruit—List C
 	
1 serving—List E
	EVENING MEAL
	1 cup fresh spinach salad with
	1 Tbsp. French dressing
	4 oz. broiled halibut garnished
	  with chopped parsley and
	  lemon slices
	½ cup steamed rice
	4 oz. broccoli spears
	1 hard roll with
	1 tsp. margarine
	½ cup sweetened rhubarb
	  with 1 Tbsp. whipped cream
		☐ *For Controlled Weight Gain follow the special instructions given in the boxes at the bottom of each of the 5 food groups.

BEDTIME
1 serving milk—List A
	BEDTIME
	1 package Carnation Instant
	  Breakfast made with Carnation
	  Instant Nonfat Milk	

SUBSTITUTION LISTS

LIST A: MILK GROUP Foods Included:

Milk — fluid whole, Carnation evaporated, fluid skim, Carnation instant nonfat milk, buttermilk, low fat milk

Cheese — cottage (1 cup = 1 cup milk); cheddar-type, natural or processed (1 oz. = ¾ cup milk)

Ice Cream

Carnation Instant Breakfast

Carnation Slender

Yogurt

Amount recommended: At least 4 eight oz. cups per day

Milk is a leading source of calcium which is needed for bones and teeth. It also provides high quality protein, riboflavin, vitamins A, D, E, B_6, B_{12}, phosphorus, magnesium, and zinc.

> *If controlled weight gain is desirable, use skim milk, Carnation Instant Nonfat Milk, low fat yogurt, cottage cheese, and Carnation Slender to fulfill the requirements of this group.

LIST B: MEAT GROUP Foods Included:

Beef; veal; lamp; pork; variety meats, such as liver, heart, kidney

Poultry and eggs

Fish and shellfish

As alternatives — dry beans, dry peas, lentils, nuts, peanuts, peanut butter

Amounts Recommended: The equivalent of at least 3 servings daily. Count as a serving: 2 to 3 ounces of lean cooked meat, poultry, or fish — all without bone.

2 eggs

1 cup dry beans, dry peas, or lentils

4 tablespoons peanut butter

Foods in this group are valued for their protein, which is needed for growth and repair of body tissues — muscles, organs, blood, skin, and hair. These foods also provide iron, thiamin, riboflavin, vitamins B_6, B_{12}, phosphorus, zinc, and iodine. Vegetable protein foods provide protein, iron, thiamin, folacin, vitamins B_6, and E, phosphorus, magnesium, and zinc.

> *If controlled weight gain is desirable, select lean cuts of meats and choose poultry and fish often. Use broiling, roasting, steaming, boiling, or baking methods of cooking and avoid the use of fats and oils in food preparation.

LIST C: VEGETABLE-FRUIT GROUP Foods Included:

All vegetables and fruits
Valuable sources of vitamin C and vitamin A are listed below:

Sources of Vitamin A: Dark green leafy and deep yellow vegetables and a few fruits, namely: Apricots, broccoli, cantaloupe, carrots, chard, collards, cress, kale, turnip greens, pumpkin, spinach, sweet potatoes, winter squash (Hubbard, acorn, etc.).

Sources of vitamin C: Good sources: Grapefruit or grapefruit juice, cantaloupe, raw strawberries, broccoli, brussels sprouts.

Fair sources: Honeydew melon, tangerine or tangerine juice, watermelon, raw cabbage, greens — collards, kale, mustard, turnip, green pepper, potatoes and sweet potatoes cooked in the jacket, spinach, tomatoes or tomato juice, fresh or frozen raspberries.

Amounts recommended: Choose 4 or more servings daily, including: 1 serving of a good source of vitamin C or 2 servings of a fair source; 1 serving, at least every other day, of a good source of vitamin A.

Count as 1 serving:
½ cup vegetable or fruit
A portion as ordinarily served such as 1 medium apple, orange, banana, or potato; ½ a medium grapefruit or cantaloupe.

Fruits and vegetables are valuable chiefly because of the vitamins and minerals they contain. In this plan, the group is counted on to supply nearly all the vitamin C needed and over half of the vitamin A.

> *If controlled weight gain is desirable, limit consumption of corn, potatoes, or sweet potatoes to 1 serving per day. Use fresh or water-pack fruits and avoid those canned with sugar.

LIST D: BREAD-CEREAL GROUP Foods Included:

All breads and cereals that are whole grain, enriched, or restored. (Brown rice and converted rice are in this group.)

Cereals, cooked or ready-to-eat, cornmeal, grits

Enriched or whole grain flour

Macaroni, spaghetti, noodles made from enriched flour

Quick breads and other baked goods if made with whole grain or enriched flour

Amounts recommended: Choose 4 servings or more daily. Count as 1 serving: 1 slice of bread, 1 ounce of ready-to-eat cereal, ½ to ¾ cup cooked cereal, cornmeal, grits, macaroni, noodles, rice, or spaghetti.

Foods in this group furnish worthwhile amounts of protein, iron, several of the B vitamins, phosphorus, zinc, and food energy.

> *If controlled weight gain is desirable, avoid the use of quick breads and other baked goods which contain large amounts of sugar, honey, or fat. Limit total number of servings in this group to 5 per day.

LIST E: OTHER FOODS

Foods other than those listed in Lists A, B, C, and D can usually be included to meet daily energy requirements and to add variety to meals. Refined breads, cereals, flours; sugars; butter; margarine, and other fats are examples. It is recommended that some vegetable oil be included among the fats used.

The use of the following is also recommended:
Iodized salt
Pasteurized milk fortified with 400 International Units of vitamin D

Foods not specifically mentioned in the food groups supply additional food energy (calories) and may add to the total nutrients in meals.

> *If controlled weight gain is desirable, avoid sugar, honey, concentrated sweets, pies, cakes, pastry, rich desserts, regular soft drinks. Limit the use of fats and oils to 2 Tbsp. per day.

You should count calories as you are reducing. After you have your weight in check and continue with the endurance exercise, a precise, daily calorie count may not be necessary. However, common sense tells you that if you ate a huge hamburger and milkshake for lunch, you had better not eat a dinner of roast beef, potatoes, and gooey dessert. Or, if you know your favorite pie ala-mode is being served at the Relief Society party, perhaps you need to eliminate desserts all week.

When I was a child, we had dessert every night after dinner. After my weight loss, I stopped that habit and found out that dessert after dinner is just that — HABIT. We have desserts on Sunday and after family home evening. That is enough to last all week. It's hard to break any habit, but what a great place to start eliminating excess daily calories.

Try a little experiment: for two days record every single morsel (no cheating!) that passes your lips. You may be surprised at the end of those two days to see how much surplus food you have eaten. Surplus food is what I call the nasty nibbles — those foods that just satisfy nerves or taste buds but really don't do very much for hunger or nutrition!

Two other ideas worth mentioning that I found helped me lose the weight and keep it off:

1. Push yourself away from the table when you are *satisfied* but do not have a "full" or "stuffed" feeling. This idea came to me one Thanksgiving Day.

It had been a great feast and I had overeaten and lay around moaning with everyone else. Then the thought consumed me: Boy, are you ridiculous! Look and listen to yourself, Anita. You could have been content two servings ago!

I had broken the Word of Wisdom, and I ached, but what dawned on me was the fact that it didn't just happen at holiday meals. There were many times each month that I ate until I felt quite full, stuffed, in fact. How often do you eat too much?

It's another HABIT to which we adjust our bodies and mouths! If you can think about your next meal (without gagging) when you leave the table, you've mastered this idea! Does it really work! It did for me. Many women who have tried it have told me it not only helped in weight control but helped them feel greater energy instead of a sluggish feeling after eating.

2. Weigh yourself every morning and evening. Once you get in control again, weighing yourself twice a week is adequate. In the beginning, however, there are two reasons to weigh yourself each morning and night: (a) it keeps the goal foremost in your mind, and you can set the plan in the morning, commit yourself to the exercise and calorie counting, and then re-evaluate your progress at night; (b) it keeps pounds from sneaking up on you. (Ever been discouraged after a vacation when you step on the scales and see a new ten pounds? Keeping a daily check allows you to do something about unwanted pounds THAT VERY DAY!)

Seventeen years ago I weighed 140 pounds with a 5'2" frame. It was easy to look in the mirror and pretend I saw Raquel Welch! Then one day I faced the "bare" facts and decided it was time to lose weight. However, the real commitment was not yet there. After a few half-hearted attempts, the repeated failures overwhelmed me. Then one particular day I made a resolution to lose the weight and NEVER be fat again. When I made the commitment, I MADE IT FOR THE REST OF MY LIFE. I have weighed 100 pounds for nearly seventeen years now, and as I have evaluated my success, I believe it was due to *knowing* I could succeed as well as being determined to do so.

Dr. Zimmerman's article clearly implies that a majority of obese women have a biochemical problem. Try as they may they find complete failure in dieting. There are many other women who simply eat too much food or too much of the wrong kinds of food. In either case, endurance exercise married with good nutrition is the answer to a better physical body. Of that, I have a personal testimony.

And whether you eat too much or starve yourself and still gain weight, one fact surfaces clearly: either you are going to do something about it, or you are not.

When I tell people that I once weighed forty-fifty pounds more than I do now, they amaze me when they ask, "How did you do it?" They mean, "How did I lose the weight?" I guess they are hoping for some miracle drug or idea I used, or maybe I rubbed pictures of beautiful women on my body — some way to get it off without pain. They always look disappointed when I answer that I didn't eat. The other thing that never ceases to amaze me is whenever I refuse a goody and someone will invariably say, "YOU?" You are so thin. You don't need to pass that up." How do they think I STAY thin? I could eat my way to hog heaven.

What has been described to you is a positive and pleasant approach to weight loss and control, but in theory and practice the success depends upon the determination and self-discipline of YOU, the one who wants to feel happy again with your appearance.

I know how awful you feel when you look in that mirror and see ugly fat. I also know how discouraged and unfeminine you feel. Satan plays on that and tells you that you might as well give up, that you are in too deep! And you believe him! You think you are forever trapped in an overweight body!

These techniques have proven successful: endurance exercise, planned calorie intake, moderation in all things, and the self-discipline to DO IT NOW. These are the keys to a more beautiful you.

Do you remember the story about the P.O.W. in 1970, who appeared on national television with Viet Cong approval? He talked, emotionless, to the American public and told them he was guilty of rape and murder of Vietnamese women and children. He said he deserved to be incarcerated and had committed other war crimes. He said he was not being tortured and was well cared for in the prison.

A close friend viewed the film. He knew something seemed wrong. His friend was thin, pale, weary looking, and kept blinking his eyes incessantly. Nevertheless, he couldn't put his finger on what it was that seemed disturbing.

Several weeks later, in the middle of the night, he bolted from a deep sleep and shouted aloud to his wife, "MORSE CODE!" The P.O.W.'s blinking eyes were sending a message in Morse Code! The message was the exact opposite of what the Viet Cong had blackmailed him to say — blackmail for the lives of his fellow prisoners. He was being tortured, and many were in need of medical help. The incident prompted a quickened effort to free the prisoners.

The greatest lesson we can learn here is that no matter what happens to our bodies, our physical counterpart to our spirits, no matter what happens to our environment, NO ONE CAN HAVE OUR MINDS. If we are determined to succeed, we *will* succeed! Remember WHO you are. You were born to *succeed*. As a daughter of God, you have a noble birthright. YOU CAN DO IT! This allotting of time for proper exercise and the conscious effort of dieting is a great test of self-discipline—mind over matter. YOU CAN do it.

Your Father in Heaven took into consideration your temporal and physical needs just as your earthly parents have done for you! There is no better nutritional counsel or advice than that found in the 89th Section of the Doctrine and

Covenants. I am personally opposed to health food fads, nutritional extremists, and weight control clinics. Participating in health food fanaticism is contrary to the Word of Wisdom. The Lord said he provided all these things (herbs, grain, fowl, flesh of beasts, etc.) "for the use of man" (D&C 89:12). The four food groups didn't just materialize out of the laboratory of some dietician. Your Heavenly Father provided these things for the good of all mankind. He then gave us brains to use these things wisely. How simple are divine things: "Yea, all things which come of the earth . . . are made for the benefit and the use of man, both to please the eye and to gladden the heart; . . . to strengthen the body and to enliven the soul" (D&C 59:18-19).

May I also add that as friends and loved ones, we have no justification in downgrading or judging others because of their weight problems. I have been so guilty of that in the past — not understanding that many women are aching inside to overcome this barrier to a better self-image. As Dr. Zimmerman explained, obesity is not always due to a lack of self-discipline. No matter what it is due to, who are we to judge each other? Instead of judging, let's help one another! Sisters, band together. Start groups committed to losing weight and keeping it lost. Befriend someone who could use your encouragement. Ask someone you admire for help. Are we not *really* sisters? Don't you want the best for your flesh-and-blood sister? Such an attitude toward all the daughters of our Heavenly Father is no less a Christlike attitude. We must indeed love one another as He loved us.

There is no greater feeling of confidence and self-esteem than that which is yours when you know your spirit has mastered your physical body. Go on. Take the challenge. Rise to the challenge for YOU CAN DO IT! You might say, "You have everything to lose and nothing to gain!"

Chapter  Three

Beauty Is Also Skin Deep

"If there is anything virtuous, lovely, or of good report or praiseworthy, we seek after these things."
—*Joseph Smith*

Every woman is beautiful whether or not her features will be claimed as "Cover Girl" material. It is of no significance if you and your face are not considered by the world as one of the B.P. (Beautiful People). Your real beauty is not of this world. As members of the Church, you have an inner beauty that makes possible an unusual outer beauty.

But what is beauty? To every woman it will mean different things and carry with it a personal list of adjectives. Certainly, the spiritual beauty is most important, but the physical beauty is a thing to be cherished. Why?

Who can explain the fresh loveliness of any child? Sun-kissed, golden tresses, a clear complexion, and bright, sparkling eyes are so bewitching on *every* child. These little children are newly arrived from a celestial home, and I have often thought how near they are to what we looked like before we came to earth. BEAUTY IS BUT THE SENSIBLE IMAGE OF GOD! Like eternal truths and laws, it lives within each of us. Ralph Waldo Emerson put it this way: "Beauty is God's handwriting . . . a wayside sacrament. Welcome it in every fair face, in every fair sky, in every fair flower, and thank God for it as a cup of blessing."

Nevertheless, as every new object eventually loses its shine and freshness, so we mortals tend to lose such traces of newness. The glamour of well-coiffed hair and a fresh, bright face have been sought after since the ancient days of Greece. I for one am thankful I live today in this world of scientific marvels! I can't imagine life without lipstick, deodorant, or curling irons! (Do you realize what our pioneer sisters would have given for hot rollers?)

The ideas and techniques on the following pages are condensed from volumnious amounts of books and material. (I know how Mormon felt!) These are the meat and potatoes of beauty techniques. I have eliminated all the "fluff" so that these constitute sensible, simple steps to a more beautiful you.

Hair

It has been said that a woman's hair is her crowning glory. Why then do so many crowns look tarnished? Almost every woman has had the experience of going to the hair dresser and then coming home less than what she considered a raving beauty. Remember standing at the mirror, hairbrush in hand, near tears if not in tears, wanting to shave your head and start over? Women want their hair to look nice, to be just right.

While recuperating from surgery this past year, I watched a woman's talk show on television. That particular afternoon the guest of honor was a highly acclaimed cosmetologist. She had called three women from the studio audience the previous week and had taken them to her salon for a "make over." As each woman stepped onto the stage with her new look, the camera flashed a "before" picture. It was unbelievable! Each woman not only looked *years* younger but brighter and much more self-confident. The main contrast and most dramatic change had to do with their hair, both in color and style. Mousy and drab color was given life, unflattering harsh gray was muted, flat blonde hair was given highlights and glow. Each woman also had her hair cut and styled to suit the shape of her face and her age. Believe me when I tell you that the contrast was remarkable. A healthy, clean, attractive hair color and hair style will give you more self-confidence than anything else you can do for yourself.

So many women want to improve their appearance by starting with their hair — either a change in color or style. However, they often end up disappointed and frustrated because (1) they've chosen a hard-to-do-yourself hair style, (2) the wrong hair style for the shape of their face, (3) they have gone to a mediocre hairdresser, or (4) they have ignored damaged or mousy hair.

Let's outline some basic steps which you should follow in order to make your hair truly your crowning glory:

1. There is nothing more unattractive than greasy, dirty hair. When I was in college, there was a coed whose hair always seemed greasy and stringy. We realized it was because she only washed her hair once a week and that since it was very oily, she needed to wash it every other day. She had simply been taught that Saturday was the day to wash hair — no other day. Here was an 18-year-old girl who was a victim of someone else's routine. She quickly learned from her friends how to keep her hair clean and shiny.

2. Read the labels on the bottle and buy as follows:
   Normal — for hair that isn't particularly oily or dry and can go several days without shampooing.

Oily — for hair that feels greasy the day after shampooing. (Shampoo every other day or daily if
necessary.)

Dry — flyaway hair, little moisture in it. (You need to
also use a creme rinse or conditioner.)

Limp or fine — needs to be shampooed every morning
with an "extra body" shampoo.

Color-treated — needs protection of a colorfast shampoo.

Scalp problems — needs a medicated shampoo. (Ask
your doctor to recommend one.)

3. More tips on the art of shampooing:
   •Lather twice, unless you shampoo daily.
   •Rinse thoroughly. (Residue dulls the hair.)
   •Use cool water for final rinse, especially if it's oily.
   •Finger comb when wet. (Brushing may cause damage
   because wet hair is very fragile.)
   •Use a creme rinse or conditioner as often as necessary
   to make hair shiny and manageable.

4. The next step is to get a decent haircut, not one from the
   neighbor or a non-practicing beautician, unless they
   happen to be current on techniques and exhibit great
   talent. Choose a reputable hairdresser. How? Never be
   afraid to ask a woman, even a stranger you see in the
   grocery store, who does her hair. When you see an excellent cut and coiffure, don't hesitate to ASK. Most women
   are flattered.

   With the high cost of beauty salons it may not be
   possible to go once a week or even once a month, so
   you must have your hairdresser help you choose a style
   not only flattering to your face but one that is easy for
   you to handle, especially as it grows out. A friend of
   mine, who really struggles financially, goes to the best

hairdresser in town. She pays the top price for the haircut, but that's all she gets, a haircut. It is such a good one however, and her style so manageable that she only goes every three months. She said that when she went to the thrift-rate salons, she needed one nearly every month!

5. Choose a flattering style. Again, a good hairdresser can help. If you pull all your hair away from your face and look in a mirror, you will see that your face has a definite shape. Thumb through several beauty magazines and try to find faces shaped like yours. Tear out the pictures, and you will see the styles probably most flattering for you. Here are a few simple descriptions:

Square Face — forehead and jaw are equal
   • Center part or long side part are ideal.
   • Neckline hair that shows from front will soften square jawline.
   • No long, straight bangs.
   • High temple area should be covered with hair.

Inverted Triangle — wide forehead, narrow jaw
   • Fullness should be around chin line.
   • A center part is most flattering.
   • Avoid short cuts — fullness at neck line adds width to jaw.

Diamond — narrow forehead and jaw, wide cheekbones
   • Create fullness ABOVE temple areas.
   • Off-center parts are ideal.
   • Keep hair close to cheekbones and full at jaw line.

Round face — full face
   • Comb hair forward towards cheek area to create *length* in face.
   • Fullness at top of head (crown) helps to balance

and add length.
- •Avoid short, close, cropped styles.

Long or Oval — long chin and forehead
- •Avoid center parts (looks longer).
- •Fullness should be at sides.
- •Wear hair shorter and fuller.
- •Bangs will soften face.

Triangle — narrow forehead, wide jaw
- •No center part.
- •Fullness at forehead (full bangs) and temple.
- •No fullness at neck or jaw.
- •Height at crown will balance face.
- •Side part a must if no bangs.

Here are some other hints:

- •Prominent nose — full bangs reduce size of nose.
- •Receding chin — fullness at neckline gives chin more balance.
- •Small face — hair should be kept back away from face.
- •Women over 35 — don't wear hair past your shoulders; it ages you.
- •Large face — comb hair toward face to minimize.
- •Pregnant or overweight women — your hair should look lovely even if you feel your body doesn't. It is important not to dispose of that part of your *good* self-image.

Once you have the right style, don't be discouraged if the first time you try it on your own, it doesn't look like it did at the salon. PRACTICE. If you have chosen an easy style, a few times on your own and it will look right.

6. Consider a permanent. Permanents will free you from

hours of hair care, and they help keep the style set and lasting. However, salon permanents are extremely expensive and often very harsh on your hair. The best one I ever had was a home permanent given to me by my mother-in-law in her kitchen.

You must read the labels, find one right for your type of hair, and follow the instructions EXACTLY. Here are some helps:

- Have a friend help you for best results.
- Is your hair hard-to-wave, easy, natural, color-treated, fragile, healthy? Choose a perm tailored to meet hair needs.
- Wide rollers for body, medium rollers for medium curl, small rollers for tight curls.
- Do not perm on badly damaged hair.
- Trim split ends first. (Your hairdresser does this.)
- Always shampoo first.
- Test your hair. (See package instructions.)
- After the perm, wait two days to shampoo and two weeks before coloring.

7. Don't be afraid of coloring your hair. After a woman turns twenty-five or has had several pregnancies, it has been scientifically established that many women have a change in their body chemistry. One of the first places that shows such changes is the hair.

If your hair looks tired, mousy, yellowed, or is in the early stages of gray, you will want to consider coloring it. The most flattering effect results from sticking to your own color and just enhancing its natural beauty.

The art of haircoloring has been made very easy for you whether you're a wife, homemaker, mother, or single working woman. There are two types of color treatment: semi-permanent and permanent.

Semi-permanent is a shampoo-in formula and lasts through four to six shampoos.

There are four types of *permanent* coloration — color that does not wash out:

Shampoo-in tints — color result is based on your own, natural color plus the shade you choose.

Creme formulas — if you are more than one-third gray or your gray resists color, this is the one for you.

Two-step blonding — step one lightens the hair, and step two adds the color blonde you want (for natural blondes only).

Special effect kits — these are for sunny highlights and accents.

Clairol has a TOLL FREE Hair Help Hotline at 1-800-223-5800. If you have any questions, call them. They are very willing to help you.

Some Tips:

Ask for advice from someone who has colored her hair.

Ask your hairdresser for suggestions but offer to pay her for her advice. She's working to make a living.

Your own haircolor is the best choice.

Don't try to be too dramatic, like wild streaking. The hair is to flatter your face, not be the main event.

8. Tricks with hair spray (courtesy of ADORN COMPANY):
For softly styled, finished looks, spray hair lightly before setting with electric rollers or a curling iron. As the temperature goes from hot to cold, the spray will act as a setting gel. The result? Lasting curl, body, and

bounce.

If you want to achieve a look of extra volume and thickness, bend over from the waist and spray the underside of your hair. Let dry and toss head back. To finish the style, finger-comb hair lightly into place.

If your braids are not lasting as long as you'd like, why not use hair spray before styling? Spray will add body and get rid of flyaway ends and will give you more control while braiding. Spray hair first, braid, then lightly mist again. Braids will stay in place for hours and sport a glimmering shine.

If your permed hair looks dull, comb hair in place while wet, spray, then finger-comb to dry. For an even shinier evening look, try using setting gel before spraying.

Stylish combs and barrettes are often difficult to keep in place. Mist with hair spray first and then experiment with different combs. They won't slip!

Mist a tissue with hair spray and hold it over flyaway ends. This also works well for the new upswept hairdos for evening.

For a finished, controlled-looking style, spray your hands and gently pat down areas where hair is "jumping."

Spray your hair brush and then run it through your hair. This will avoid static electricity and break down a really tight set.

Skin

Color analysis is the process by which each person's skin

coloring is put into one of four categories: autumn, winter, spring, or summer. Back in the 1950s it was assumed that you couldn't go wrong in basic black and pearls. Then someone said, "Hey, I look awful in black," and the eyebrows were raised. A study was done at UCLA, and it was determined that each person falls into only one skin tones group.

Different colors were then established to be complementary to these separate skin tones, and they fell into the colors of each of the seasons:

Autumn	Winter	Spring	Summer
orange	purple	coral	pale gray
rust	black	royal blue	pastel pink
olive green	white	camel	baby blue
forest green	hot pink	bright red	mint green
gold	pure red	lime green	soft (grayed) yellow

The important thing to remember is that any person can wear any color! The secret to colorization is whether or not your season shade has been added to the color:

Autumn
Brown must be added to the color to produce muted shades.

Winter
Pure color — nothing added.

Spring
White is added so that colors are very bright.

Summer
Gray is added so that colors become pastel or grayed.

I am an autumn, but I can wear pink if it has brown added to it so as to make it a brownish-rose color. A spring can wear orange if it has white added to it to make it coral. Summer can wear yellow if gray is added to it to make it pastel yellow. Winter wears pure white and other pure colors.

Isn't that simple? The color experts won't tell you these principles; it doesn't sell books or classes. Once you open your eyes and train yourself to look, you can recognize the shade in any color.

Color analysis should be done by a person trained in this field. To guess by yourself may result in a wrong conclusion. The cost for such an analysis presently ranges anywhere from $5 to $150, depending on where you live and where you choose to have it done. Many consultants do it in their home and charge an average of $25 to $30. Salons will charge much more. Without color analysis you have (statistically) one chance in four that you will pick the correct colors to wear. However, haven't you had the experience of trying on a dress and thinking: "This color looks awful on me"? Or maybe you have noticed that when you wear a certain color, you receive more compliments?

Color analysis not only provides you with clothing colors but information on make-up and hair color best suited to each group. Winter and summer have warm skin tones and need to be cooled down by wearing cool colors. Spring and autumn have cool skin tones and need warming up by the wearing of warm shades.

You should wear "your colors" near your face and then you can wear any other color from other groups for skirts, pants, jackets, etc. For a striking look, however, it's best to wear your colors head to toe.

Color analysis is also a money saver. You need never again have a dress that gathers dust in the closet while you wonder why you bought it. It probably wasn't your color. Clothes will become an investment. You can start with basics and add on year after year, confident in the correct color choice.

I wish to thank another friend, Nadine Roempel, for the

following descriptions of the four seasons. She is an expert color analyst and was very willing to share her outlines with you.

Autumn

1. COLORS
   Teal blue
   Periwinkle
   Turquoise
   Earth greens (olive, moss, forest)
   Oyster white
   Earth beiges, gold-tone beiges
   Camel
   Most browns, especially dark brown
   All oranges
   Deep peach, salmon, rust
   Orange reds, tomato
   All golds
   No black or navy

2. PERSONALITY
   Tempermental, positive, sure in movement (firm in step), likes emotional outlet beyond home. (Nine out of ten women in business are autumn.) Rather be fervidly wrong than tepidly right. Decisions are made quickly. Likes to look smart instead of pretty. Strong features.

3. PROTOTYPES
   Katherine Hepburn
   Lauren Bacall
   Shirley Maclaine
   Carol Burnett
   Lucille Ball
   Eve Arden

Ingrid Bergman
Joan Crawford
Rhonda Fleming
Deborah Kerr

4. HAIR COLOR
Golden blonde
Golden brown
Red brown
Red
Strawberry
Cover gray unless hair is completely gray.

5. FOUNDATION MAKE-UP
Use a yellow-base foundation (ask salesgirl).
Use ivory, peach, or copper tones.
A sallow autumn does best with a peach.

6. LIPSTICK (REVLON BRAND NAME)
Corals
   Coral Vanilla
Golden Oranges
   Orange Flip
   Orange Sherbet
Tangerine Sherbet
   Mango Sherbet
Russets
   Molcha Polka
   Cinnamon Stick
   Toffee Sherbet
Avante Garde
   Blase Apricot
   Nouveau Peach
Frosted
   Florentine Gold

Apricot Ice
Butter Pecan

7. HOSIERY (HANES)
South Pacific
Topaz
Paprika
Town Taupe
Soho

8. PERFUMES
The Forest Scents
Filigran — House of 4711
Golden Autumn — Matchabelli
Evening in Paris — Bourjois
Tweed — Yardley
Chantilly — Houbigant
Desert Flower — Shulton
LaTabae Blond — Caron
Mitsouko — Guerlain
Stradivari — Matchabelli
Apropos — Anjou
Spicy
Scandal — Lanvin
Pirat — House of 4711
L'Origan — Coty
Woodhue — Faberge
20 Carats — Dana
L'Air Du Temps — Nina Ricci
Intoxication — D'Orsey
Gay Diversion — Evyan
Zizane — Corday
Odalisque — Rosenstein

Winter

1. COLORS
   Shocking pink and hot pink
   Magenta
   Fuchsia
   True reds and blue reds
   Burgundy
   Lemon Yellow
   Royal Purple
   Violet
   Pure White
   Pure Black
   Taupe
   Charcoal gray
   Navy and royal blue
   Emerald green
   No tan or gold

2. PERSONALITY
   Aloof (may seem snobbish), usually a perfectionist, appearance in itself is a design, should keep everything simple, things added take away from winter, would rather do things yourself and not depend on others, a watcher of others, gives appearance of regality, striking.

3. PROTOTYPES
   Cher
   Elizabeth Taylor
   Ava Gardner
   Marie Osmond
   Sally Field
   Audrey Hepburn
   Jacqueline Onassis

Jaclyn Smith
Hedy Lamar

4. HAIR COLOR
Ash brown
Blue-black
If gray, no need to color (even if partially gray)

5. FOUNDATION MAKE-UP
Rose base (ask salesgirl)
Rose, pink, sand, natural beige

6. LIPSTICK (REVLON)
Reds
   Brave
   Love That Red
   Queen of Diamonds
   Certainly Red
Shocking Pink
   Lilac Champagne
   Pinkissimo
Frosted
   Platinum

7. HOSIERY (HANES)
Quick Silver
Barely Black
Town Taupe
Nymph

8. PERFUMES
Orientals
   Tabu — Dana
   Hope — Frances Denny
   Zen — Shiseido
   Yram — Mary Chess

Beloved — Matchabelli
Tigress — Faberge
Shalimar — Guerlain
Dioraum — Dior
Danger — Cire
Russian Leather — Chanel
Poivre — Caron
Toujoure Moi — Corday

Spring

1. COLORS
   Ivory
   Clear and Creamy beiges
   Camel
   Warm grays
   Tan
   Light navy
   Royal blue
   Periwinkle
   Aqua
   Turquoise
   Yellow greens
   Pale oranges
   Apricot, peach, salmon, peachy pinks
   Corals
   Rust
   Clear reds
   Bright yellow
   Blue-violet
   No black or burgandy

2. PERSONALITY
   Easy to get along with, laughs easily, gets acquainted

easily, always ready to pick up and go, very seldom temperamental, enjoys hot weather, youthful, hospitable, inner gaiety.

3. PROTOTYPES
   Joan Kennedy
   Zsa Zsa Gabor
   Julie Andrews
   June Allyson
   Doris Day
   Debbie Reynolds
   Betsy Palmer
   Dinah Shore

4. HAIR COLOR
   Flaxen Blonde
   Golden Blonde
   Golden Brown
   Red Brown
   Strawberry
   Cover gray unless all gray

5. FOUNDATION MAKE-UP
   Yellow base (ask salesgirl) in light to dark peach
   Avoid blue-pinks

6. LIPSTICK (REVLON)
   Clear Reds
      Million Dollar Red
      Fire and Ice
      Louis XIV Red
   Corals
      Persian Melon
      Hot Coral
      Snow Peach

      Pango Peach
      Jungle Peach
   Pinks
      Honey Vanilla
      Pink Vanilla
      Strawberry Vanilla
      Honey Bee Pink
      Avant Garde (name changed)
   Avant Garde
      Bare Beige
      Swinging Pink
      Beach Peach
      Pink-Cognito
   Frosted
      Sugar Peach
      Sugar Blonde

7. HOSIERY (HANES)
   Lotus
   Shell
   Naturelle
   High Tea

8. PERFUMES
   The Fruited Bough
      Laughter — Montail
      Femme Du Jour — Corday
   The Brilliants
      My Sin — Lanvin
      Intimate — Revlon
      Chamade — Guerlain
      Eve Reve — Rigaud
      Hypnotique — Max Factor
      Possession — Corday

Elan — Coty
Number 5 — Chanel
Estee — Estee Lauder
Rortue — Polly Bergen
Crown Jewel — Matchabelli
Quadrille — Balenciaga

Summer

1. COLORS
Soft white
Rose — beiges
Blue grays
Rosy browns
Powder blues
Periwinkle blue
Sky blue
Pastel aqua
Pastel green and yellow
Pastel pinks
Plum, rose, blue pinks
Raspberry, blue reds
Burgundy, maroon
Mauve, orchid, lavender
No black

2. PERSONALITY
Usually beautiful hand, often excels in activities using hands in a downward motion, relaxed manner, soft voice (diplomatic, carefully weighs before answering), never shouts in expressing self, extremely feminine and graceful in movement.

3. PROTOTYPES
Farrah Fawcett

Loretta Young
Spring Byington
Cheryl Tiegs
Deborah Kerr
Candace Bergen
Carol Lynley
Princess Grace of Monaco

4. HAIR COLOR:
Ash Blonde
Ash Brown
Frosted
If gray, no need to color even if only partially gray

5. FOUNDATION MAKE-UP
Rose base (ask salesgirl)
Tones of rachel, rose, sand (pink cast)

6. LIPSTICKS (REVLON)
Blue Reds
    Red Caviar
    Chaerries a la mode
    Berry Bon Bon
    Cherries in the Snow
Fuchsias
    Raspberry Icing
    Violet Icing
    Pink Lightning
Pinks
    Pink Heaven
    Powder Pink
    Love That Pink
    Sphinx Pink
    Butterfly Pink
    Snow Pink

Paint the Town Pink
Avant Garde
  Naked Pink
  Madly Mauve
  Low Down Pink
  Super-Natural
Frosted
  Pink Coconut
  Pink Cloud
  Rose God
  Sugar Mauve

7. HOSIERY (HANES)
Bali-Rose
Barely There
Nude

8. PERFUMES
Flowering Scents
  White Shoulders — Evyan
  Bellogia — Caron
  Number 22 — Chanel
  Wind Song — Matchabelli
  Great Lady — Evyan
  Tianne — Rosenstein
  Blue Grass — Elizabeth Arden
  Caleche — Hermes
  Le De — Givenchy
  T — Yves St. Laurent
  Femme — Rochas
  Arpege — Lanvin
  Joy — Jean Patou
  Climat — Lancome
  Crepe De Chine — Millot

Bed Lilac — Lentheric
April Violets — Yardley
Magic — Lancome

Mood List for the Four Seasons

Autumn	Winter	Spring	Summer
Earth Shades	*Pure Chroma*	*Light, Clear*	*Softened Color*
Dynamic	Striking	Animated	Soft-spoken
Boundless energy	Majestic	Radiant	Ladylike
Physical	Restrained	Fresh	Dreamy
Positive	Calm	Sunny	Shy
Opinionated	Tranquil	Cheerful	Timid
Strong	Undisturbed	Exuberant	Romantic
Daring	Placid	Talkative	Other era
Dashing	Controlled	Optimistic	Picturesque
Brisk	Selective	Casual	Cultured
Latin	Friends	Provincial	Refined
Flamboyant	Closed	Country look	Elegant
Showy	Classic	Spontaneous	Poise
Fiery	Smooth	Flowery	Calm
Colorful	Sharp outline	Adventuresome	Quiet
Leader	Precise	Gets involved	Elongated
Spirited	Clearly expressive	Youthful	Fragile
Rich	Organized	Captivating	Restful
Deep	Stark	Counsel	Prefers to be led
Mellow	Perfectionist	Creatures	Dependent
Anchored	Stunning	Salesman	Defers decisions
Mature	Impressive	Pretty	Limited confidence
Profound	Bookish	Like spring	Meticulous
Assured	Intellectual	All-American	Feminine
Confident	Formal	Outgoing	Slow motion
Stability	Dignified	Go-getter	Idealistic
Solid, firm	Stately	Warm	Organized
Direct	Expensive	Friendly	Sensitive
Sharp	Quality	Uncomplicated	Distinguished
Commanding	Important	Buoyant	Deeply analytical
Opulent	Extreme	Flirtatious	Self-critical

Autumn	**Winter**	**Spring**	**Summer**
Earth Shades	*Pure Chroma*	*Light, Clear*	*Softened Color*
Affluent	Lavish	Fun-loving	Deeply spiritual
Exotic	Distinguished	Frolicsome	Extreme creativity
Devastating	High fashion look	Tease	Philosophical
Textured		Perky	Graceful
Ethnic		Humorous	Flowing
			Deep highs and lows

Make-up

President McKay is reported to have said, when asked by the Brethren if Mormon women should wear make-up, "Well, even an old barn looks better when it's painted!"

A darling young woman in her middle thirties had never worn any make-up. She was dressed fairly attractively, and her hair was clean and well kept. Nevertheless, she looked washed out, pale, and just plain blah. She said her husband liked the "fresh young look." Well, so do I! But, ladies, let's be reasonable! Ater fifteen years of marriage and six children, it just wasn't there! You can't expect to look at thirty or forty or fifty like you did at sixteen. Even by the time you are in your middle twenties, that lustre and fresh color has faded from your face. This young sister had lovely features and nice eyes. A little color on her cheeks and lips would have given her sparkle and would have enhanced those eyes and face.

A lot of men (and women) have the idea that make-up makes you look cheap or detracts from the "natural" beauty God gave women. I have to agree with that wholeheartedly but only when the woman who is wearing it has used it improperly. There is nothing that detracts more from a woman's appearance (that includes girls, too!) than glaring make-up. However, when used properly, nothing can do more to enhance and accentuate your best features. This attitude of make-up cheapening an appearance

102

is just an excuse.

The most frequent excuse though is TIME. Women will say, "I don't have time to put on make-up." Time is a valuable commodity, and it is something everyone has EXACTLY the same amount of. There are sixty seconds in a minute, sixty minutes in an hour, and twenty-four hours in a day. No one has more or less than anyone else. So what the excuse really means is this: "I don't *allow* the time for it." To put on a complete "face" takes no more than five to ten minutes. Certainly the first few times you experiment it will take a lot longer, but after the technique is mastered, you can do it in five to ten minutes. Five to ten minutes is all you are away from a better self-image. Isn't that small investment in time worth that to you? It is to me. Even if a day only consists of duties around the home, you feel so much more effective if you KNOW your appearance matches that spirit.

Another excuse is this: "I have more important things to do." What a tenuous excuse! If the Lord didn't think personal appearance was important, our missionaries in the field could wear jeans, sneakers, and have long hair. They are on an important errand, yet they *allow* the time to look nice. You are on an errand, too, for life in mortality is really the Lord's errand. You are an ambassador of the Lord here upon the earth. Please *allow* the time to look like an ambassador.

An excuse is an excuse, a method of convincing yourself that you are justified in taking the path of least resistance.

In the years during which I have given classes on grooming and make-up, two obvious facts have surfaced. The classes are always jammed — WOMEN CARE. The second fact became apparent to me soon after the first — THEY DON'T TRY BECAUSE THEY DON'T KNOW HOW. Part of that comes from not wanting others to disapprove — the fear of not fitting in. The important thing to remember is that no two of us are exactly alike. Therefore, our beauty is as individual a thing as we are. You are a beautiful creation, and you should enhance that beauty.

Where To Go For Help and What To Buy

There are so many products on the market, and styles seem to change daily. What's a woman to do?

Once a year I attend a free make-up session at one of the local department stores. Large cosmetic companies and their representatives into the stores periodically stand by the sales counter with their kits and give complimentary make-up lessons. This helps sell their product, promotes good will, and generates sales. It's a great gimmick for them and even better for you.

Mr. Blackwell, a famous fashion designer, said once that he could tell what year a woman graduated from high school by her hair style and make-up. Make-up styles change just as clothing and hair styles do. Attending free clinics helps keep you abreast of current trends. That's not to say that you need to run out and buy everything new, either.

I haven't changed my make-up technique in four years because it is still subtle enough that it is stylish and attractive. Last year I went to a lesson with a friend, and the cosmetic representative gave us the latest look. It was gorgeous. However, there was just one problem; the minute I opened my mouth or moved a muscle, the "look" was over! It was perfect as long as I didn't even blink, but the moment I put animation into my face I looked quite a bit like a modern, circus performer. So, some "dramatic" effects are great for the cover of *Vogue*, but for your kitchen or for the Relief Society social they just look rather "put on." Nevertheless, even with the overdone effect, I learned something at that session. I learned a new trick to highlighting the eyes. Learning such things is a good reason for going to such sessions, for once you know the basics, you may pick up some hints here and there that will help you improve upon those basics. I have usually come away from such demonstrations with something new, and my general overall "look" has taken subtle changes. It's those subtle changes that keep you from looking as you did the year you graduated from high school.

Now, even though the demonstrations are complimentary, they do try to sell you all the products they've used, and the bill can add up quickly. Do not be intimidated by this. I usually buy one item, the one that has been used in the new technique I learned, or I buy the least expensive product; and if I don't need it, I'll give it away as a gift later or put it into my year's storage of supplies. (Did you ever think about make-up in your home storage inventory?) Such small items can be bought for three to ten dollars, and I figure that that is an inexpensive investment for a year's worth of glamour. You may like the products so well that you buy a lot more, but it's not necessary.

Make-up lasts a long time. I'm still on a bottle of foundation that I bought over one year ago, and my blusher is going on two years, and the eyeshadows are over three years old. When you buy, you want to buy right the first time. Otherwise, you find years later that you've accumulated a drawer or box full of half-used blushers, lipsticks, shadows, etc. They never seemed right, did they? And you kept switching products until the extent of your investment might compete with that of a door-to-door cosmetic salesman.

Let me share with you a few little tips I have learned that have kept me out of the "buy it again" syndrome.

Understand Your Skin Color.

Everyone has underlying color tones of pink, yellow, gray, beige, etc. (See section on color analysis.) For example, I have a very sallow cast (yellow) to my skin. If I wear beige foundation, it turns gray on my skin. Pink foundations turn reddish. So I use golden (bronze) or peach, and that corrects the yellow color in my skin. How do you know what cast your skin has? A make-up specialist can tell you. Where are they? The sales representative that I've already mentioned, usually a good beauty salon employs one, and there are plenty of make-up shops (Merle Norman, Elizabeth Arden, etc.) in malls and shopping centers that also will help you. This service is usually complimentary, but it is nice to buy at least a small item. After you understand your skin color, you'll use one bottle until it's gone, so there will be no waste. The color will be perfect for you. You must also remember the colorization group you belong to: spring, summer, winter, or autumn. Eyeshadow colors, lipsticks, and blushers should be coordinated. You don't want to wear blue shadow, rust blush, and pink lipstick. A better blend would be brown shadow, rust blush, and copper lipstick.

Understand Your Skin Type.

Do you have oily, dry, or normal skin, or a combination? For example: mine is oily, so I wear water-base foundation, powder shadows, powder blushers, and waterproof mascara. Oil base make-ups, after a few hours, seem to slide right off my face! The powders stay. If you have dry or normal skin, oil-base foundations are the ones for you, and you can use cream shadows and blushers. Knowing this about yourself will prevent wasted money.

What To Buy.

The cosmetic counter is often a journey into complete confusion. There is a smorgasbord of make-up: make-up for over make-up, make-up for under make-up, make-up for day and make-up for evening, make-up for every color, "stuff" to take it off with, "stuff" to put it on with, and "stuff" to make your own! If budget is your concern and you think you can't afford make-up, you might be glad to know that with the right purchases, it can cost you ten dollars or less per year (at this printing).

First of all, soap is soap, and fancy make-up and skin cleansers do not clean your face any better than soap. Any idea to the contrary is a false image painted (no pun intended) by the cosmetic industry. I spoke to a prominent dermatologist, and he told me that cleaning make-up off the face is better done with cool water, mild soap, and a little vaseline for the eyes.

A basic make-up wardrobe should consist of these items:

1. Bottle of foundation
2. Blusher
3. Mascara
4. Eyeshadow — basic color (You can add other colors later.)
5. Lipstick
6. Highlighter — (white if you are summer or winter, cream if you are autumn or spring)
7. Eyebrow pencil
8. Tweezer
9. Eyelash curler

Deleting the eyelash curler (about three dollars) and a pair of tweezers (about $2.50), which are one-time purchases, the cost of these items (at a local discount store for commonly known brands) are as follows:

Foundation	$ 3.75
Blusher	3.45
Mascara	2.35
Eyeshadow	2.25
Lipstick	2.50
Highlighter	1.75
Eyebrow Pencil	1.25
	$17.30

This supply, used daily, will last nearly two years, perhaps longer, depending on your activities. So your average expense is less than ten dollars a year. Sometimes make-up goes on sale, and I buy an extra pencil or bottle and put it in my storage. (I consider my appearance to be part of my personal welfare.) Also, as you get an extra couple of dollars, you can add to the basics with colors of shadow, lipsticks, and perhaps another color of blusher.

Color Coordinate Make-up.

Make-up should blend with the clothes you are wearing (see section on color analysis) just as it should blend with your skin coloring. Hopefully the clothes you wear will also blend with your skin coloring. Make-up, skin, and clothes are all related. The make-up itself should be coordinated. Within your color group are sets of colors (for clothes) which you can wear and so your make-up can change according to your attire.

Autumn

Rust dress	Brown shadow	Brown dress	Brown shadow
Brown dress	Rust blusher	Red dress	Brown-red blusher
Beige dress	Copper lipstick	Beige dress	Brown-red lipstick

Summer

Pink dress	Gray or mauve shadow	Green dress	Peach-green shadow
Blue dress	Rose Blusher	Pale yellow dress	Peachy pink blusher
Silver dress	Pink lipstick	Pastel peach dress	Peach lipstick

Winter

Black dress	Dark gray shadow	Navy dress	Plum & pink shadow
White dress	Burnished red blusher	Hot pink dress	Rose pink blusher
Red dress	Clear red lipstick	Burgundy dress	Deep rose lipstick

Spring

Royal blue dress	Smokey blue shadow	Apricot dress	Apricot-brown shadow
Green dress	Coral blusher	Ivory dress	Deep apricot blusher
Turquoise dress	Coral lipstick	Camel dress	Peach lipstick

Easy Make-up Tips

Eyes

First determine your eye shape, depth, spacing:

1. *Shape* — Hold a pencil horizontally across the bridge of your nose so that it passes from the inside to the outside corner of the eye. If the pencil is straight, your eyes have no slant. If the pencil slants up, you have oval or almond-shaped eyes. If the pencil slants down, your eyes droop.

2. *Depth* — Notice the amount of upper lid showing between the crease and the lash line. If a lot of lid space shows, eyes are deep set. If little or no lid shows, eyes are shallow or flat.

3. *Spacing* — Rest one end of a pencil against the base of the right side of your nose. Line it up vertically with the inside corner of your right eye. If the pencil is straight, your eyes are regularly spaced. If the pencil slants toward the bridge of your nose, your eyes are close-set. If the pencil slants outward, your eyes are set wide apart.

Having determined the shape, depth, and spacing of your eyes, here are some suggestions on how to achieve shadows and highlights:

1. *Deep-set Eyes* — Apply a light color shadow over the entire eyelid. Don't extend it above the lid. Avoid dark shades. Use narrow eyeliner above the upper lashes.

2. *Slanted or Almond-Shaped Eyes* — Apply eyeliner in a narrow line along the upper lashes from corner to corner and widen at the outer end. Line the outer half of the lower lashes. Arch your brow as much as possible. Use light shadow above the upper lashes (on

the lid), darker shadow along the lid crease, light shadow again on the brow bone.

3. *Close-set Eyes* — Apply pale shadow only on the inside half of the lid. Line the outer half of the upper and lower lashes — smudge. Arch the brow as much as possible and apply two coats of mascara to the outer half of the lashes.

4. *Small Eyes* — Place dark shadow on the outer half of the lids extending above and beyond the lids (over corner and up past lid crease). Apply a pale shadow on the inner half of the lids. Line the outer and lower half of the lashes, using two coats of mascara on the outer corners of the upper lashes.

5. *Flat Eyes with Little Lid Showing* — Avoid having brows too thick (pluck). Cover the upper lid with a pale shadow — darker shadow along the eyelid crease — and apply a pale shadow over the inner corner of the eyes. Add two coats of mascara to the outer corner of the lashes.

To make lashes look lush and thick: (1) use a lash-builder mascara, (2) put on a thin coat first (let dry a few seconds), (3) apply a heavier, more generous second coat, (4) always do the bottom lashes, too.

To make the whites of the eyes sparkle and add depth to the eyes and height to the cheekbones (contour to the face), use highlighter under the eye and sweep it towards the temple. Blend it evenly. Never let it be obvious.

Eyebrows should be plucked meticulously:
1. Never pluck from above, but always from the brow-bone, and under the natural arch.
2. The pencil (a full shade lighter than hair color) should be applied in short, feathery strokes.

3. Length is determined by the edge of the nose for the inside and the end of the brow and the corner of the eye for the outside.

4. Keep brows a shade or two lighter than your hair color. You can have very dark brows bleached and pale ones darkened with a pencil.

To make the *whites of the eyes* sparkle and to add depth, use a turquoise or real blue above and below the outer corner of the eye and then blend.

Blue- or green-eyed women should never use a *shadow* that matches their eyes. Green shadow over green eyes (or blue over blue) dulls the natural color of the eyes and detracts. All you see is shadow. Brown is the exception. Brown eyes allow the wearing of nearly every color because they are so dark.

Eyeliner should be used purely to make lashes look thicker, not to reshape the eye. Instead of the traditional black or brown liner, some women are opting for crayons and pencils, in a variety of colors, to brighten up the eyes. When putting on liner, look down into a mirror held at chin level. Do not bring the point of the brush or pencil directly towards the eye. Hold the pencil sideways, touch it to the base of your lashes, and gently draw it along, using the lash base as a guide. Start and end where lashes grow. Completely rimming the eyes can make them appear smaller.

If you wear glasses, choose a frame color close to your hair color. This eliminates extra tones around the face.

Lips

To make *lips* look fuller, outline them with a darker shade and use a lighter shade for the inside. Make the application with a lipstick brush as it makes for a more even application, better contouring.

Apply make-up sparingly around the eyes, but DO use a black, purple, or blue under-eye pencil to rim the bottom of the eye.

Cheeks (Blushers)

Never choose the pale shade in the container. They look like nothing on the cheeks. Go for the darkest colors in the packages.

To slim cheekbones and make the face look more oval, sweep the blush high on the cheekbone and then up along the hairline.

To make a fuller face and add contour to a "flat face," pucker the lips and notice the cavity created. Put the blusher at the top of the cavity (below the cheekbone) and sweep to the earlobes.

Never bring the blusher closer to the nose than the middle of the eye. Also, never bring the blusher right up against the eye.

Never use the blusher so that it looks like a round blob.

A little blush blended on the forehead and chin adds contour and depth to the face and brightens the eyes.

Foundation

To choose the correct foundation after you have determined your shade (see color analysis), match the foundation to your jaw, NOT to your cheek. The jaw line is a lighter color than your cheeks. Foundation should blend or disappear at the jawline. NEVER put it on the neck!

Using the tips and advice on the preceding pages, apply make-up in the following order:

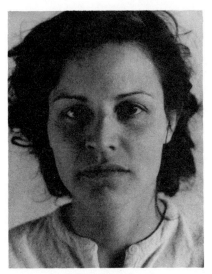

1. Start with a clean face.

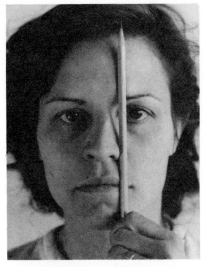

2. Determine the correct length of eyebrows.

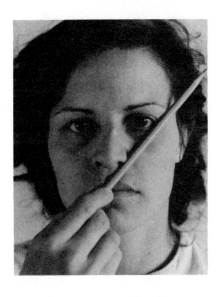

3. Determine the correct depth of eyes.

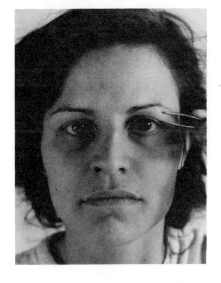

4. Pluck eyebrows.

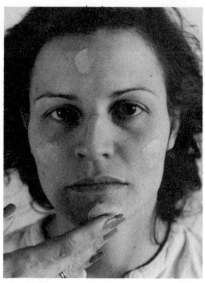

5. Apply foundation evenly over face.

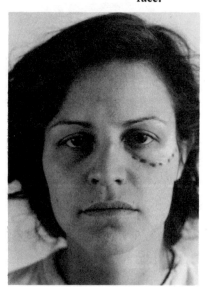 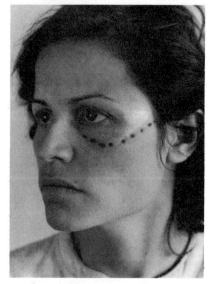

6. Use highlighter under eye and near temple to add contour to face.

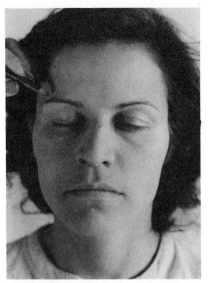

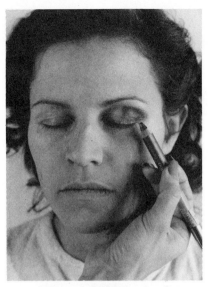

7. Apply eyebrow pencil in short, feathery strokes.

8. Apply eyeshadow according to eye type and blend evenly.

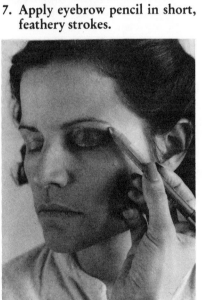

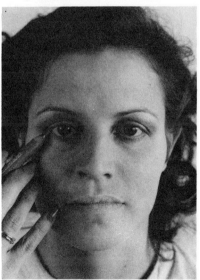

9. Apply lighter color high-lighter for accent on brow bone and blend evenly.

10. Use a smudge pencil near the lashes under the eye.

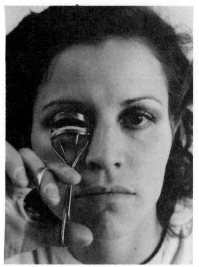

11. Curl the upper eyelashes.

12. Apply mascara—two thin coats—to both upper and lower lashes.

13. Apply blusher to cheekbone area.

14. Use a lipstick brush to outline lips with darker color.

15. Fill in the center with a lighter color.

16. Voila!

Here is Candy Krausman, wonderful friend, busy wife and mother, and great believer in the pursuit of excellence. She demonstrates the depth your face can have (and needs) with make-up when you wear glasses.

Before

After

Here is Lynn White, also an interior designer with our firm. (What these gals do for the boss!) She demonstrates differences between no make-up, too much make-up, and just enough make-up.

NO MAKE-UP	TOO MUCH	JUST RIGHT
She has nice features but looks pale and tired. There is no contrast to the lips or the cheek area. She looks plain.	The eyebrows are too heavy. Shadow needs blending. Rouge is too far forward on the cheek and too heavy. The lips have no contour, and the color on the lips is too dark.	The eyes sparkle and seem larger. Her smile is accentuated. She looks intelligent and has a quality of softness.

More Easy Tips

1. Remove all make-up at night for a fresh face in the morning.
2. Apply make-up thoroughly, i.e., to each area of the face. (I see a lot of women with lovely make-up and NO lipstick.)

3. Most women have trouble applying eye make-up but practice is the answer. In no time at all you'll be able to put it on like a professional.
4. Use a quick, glamorous hair treatment for the evening such as combing Body Glitter through your hair.
5. Take advantage of free make-up sessions at the department stores.
6. Prevent broken eyelashes by removing eye make-up with baby oil.
7. Dusting with translucent face powder helps "set" make-up and prevent smearing.
8. A moustache can be lightened with facial bleach or removed temporarily with wax or a hair remover.

THE HARD AND FAST RULES

1. Always blend your foundation along the neck and hair-lines. Never be caught with it streaked.
2. Be meticulous about keeping the eyebrows plucked.
3. Blend eyeshadows and highlighters! BLEND, BLEND, BLEND. Do not let the lines show.
4. Use baby blue, turquoise, or other bright blue and green shadows for *highlighting only!*
5. Always wear lipstick. It adds life to a face.
6. Coordinate colors of shadow, blush, and lipstick.
7. Make-up should enhance the features. If all you see is the make-up, you've overdone it.
8. Always wear mascara on the lower as well as the upper lid.

Free Beauty Advice

Merle Norman Studios offer free beauty consultations and skin care lessons. The toll free number for one near you is (800) 421-2010.

Free advice on hair, skin, or make-up problems can be

obtained from L'Oreal Consumer Hotline. The toll free number is (800) 631-7358.

Clairol Hair Color Hotline gives you personalized home hair coloring information. Their toll free number is (800) 223-5800.

Glemby Salons offer free haircuts and beauty treatments. They also tour the country demonstrating new techniques and need over 100 women to model for each week-long session. To find out when this is happening in your area, write to:

Glemby International
Public Relations Department
120 East 16th Street
New York, New York 10003

Each time I have helped a woman redo her make-up or have given advice on how to wear it, I am always met with the same reaction: "Oh! It's not me!" and I always say, "You're right! It's the NEW you!" Of course, it's an adjustment when you've been pale and plain, but I extract a promise from them, the same promise I want you to give me now. If you don't make me this promise, it won't work. You'll put on the make-up and be afraid. Promise me, please promise me, you will wear it, as outlined, every day for one week. At the end of that week, if you don't feel better about the make-up and how you look, quit wearing it. (Within three days, they always tell me they love it.) Most women are convinced. I love you. I want to see those eyes sparkle, those lips glow, those faces shine. A good painting is enhanced by its frame. A little polish on your lovely faces will make the inner beauty shine!

Personal Hygiene

Upon entering a room to give a seminar, I have often been approached and asked, in whispered tones: "Could you please

120

mention something about brushing teeth and keeping clean? I brought a friend with me who really has this problem."

No matter how much we do to look great, if we aren't clean, fresh, and good smelling, the beauty treatments are quickly spoiled. Only recently I met a beautiful woman in a beautiful ensemble whose body odor almost wilted my silk flower.

There is no substitute for soap, shampoo, deodorant, and toothpaste. Brush your teeth often, and if you doubt that your breath is pleasant, use a breath freshner, one you can keep in your purse.

Do you know the difference between anti-perspirant and deodorant? Anti-perspirant prevents perspiration, blocks the glands, and keeps wetness to a minimum. Deodorant prevents underarm odor. Sometimes you need a product that does *both*. Your personal body chemistry will let you know.

Furthermore, particular attention needs to be paid to menstrual or vaginal discharge odors. For some women the problem is minimal, but for others it is monumental. There are products (douches) on the market to help you. Consult your doctor before you buy or use such products. My doctor recommends a home douche mixture of one quart water and two tablespoons vinegar.

Other areas of the body such as hands, feet, ears, neck, and elbows need cleaning or grooming to remain soft and attractive and add to your feminine appearance.

Once you understand some basics about yourself, you can have a lot of enjoyment on just a few dollars, and you'll keep getting better. Notice I said "better." You are beautiful just because you are a daughter of God. We must realize that change is an integral part of progress. While change doesn't always mean progress, there is no progress without necessary change!

There is no need to be afraid of change. The story is told of a wealthy matron who hired a well-known photographer to take her picture every five years. She was pleased until her 60th birthday. She stormed in to his office, marched to his desk, and threw the proofs at him.

"This picture," she shouted, "isn't nearly as good as the one you took five years ago!"

"Well," he graciously replied, "I'm not the man I was five years ago. And you, Madam, are not the woman you were five years ago, either!"

Let me share with you a refreshing story about a woman I met at one of the seminars.

As everyone filed in and took their seats, I noticed a woman, in her fifties, who came in and sat towards the middle isle, her clothes were jeans, a sleeveless, quilted parka, and hiking boots. She was close enough to me that I could see every expression on her face. Her entire posture and countenance echoed: "I DARE YOU! I've read it all. Teach me IF YOU CAN."

She sat quietly through the first workshop. During the second one, which is on the physical you, she continually shook her head negatively. As I looked at her, I silently said, "Father, she's HERE. She came. Please, if there's something you want her to know, let the Spirit tell her here."

The workshops progressed, and as soon as the closing prayer was said, she headed straight for the door. I thought she was a lost cause. The following day I repeated the seminar for a new group of women, and as they filed in, here came that same sister. As I watched her through that second session, she came right up to me and said, "Yesterday, when you spoke, I kept telling myself that I wasn't the type."

"I know that!" I thought. "All last evening," she continued, "I kept having these feelings stirred in my heart. Then the little voice said, 'You have seven sons; how are you teaching them what a woman is?' and I knew that part of my partnership with God was with my mother in heaven, too."

My bottom lip started to tremble.

"Anita," she said, "will you stay ten minutes and put make-up on me, please, please will you? I've never worn it, but now I know and I can and should and would look better. I want to be more of a woman."

At that point my whole spirit trembled.

A few sisters stayed and watched, and when all the OOHS and AHS were quieted down, she looked up at me and said, "The shoes need to go, too?"

"Oh, my, yes!"

"I knew you would say that! But it's okay because I have always wanted to be lovely. I was just afraid."

Chapter  Four

The Great Put-On

"It is very unrealistic to assume that the clothes we wear and the appearance we are satisfied with have no effect upon the course of our lives. They do."

—*Barbara B. Smith*

What is discussed in this chapter is a simple and sensible approach to dressing more effectively. The examples and specifics are not intended to offend anyone, only to teach. It isn't possible, I suppose, to approach this subject without causing some women to feel uncomfortable. After all, it's personal taste we are holding up to review. Most women, however, choose incorrectly because they simply don't know any better. What is important is that you learn how to avoid mistakes and that you learn to look and feel more confident.

Clothes have to be investments, particularly as inflation sends the prices higher and higher. The most expensive dress in your closet is the one you never wear. (If you estimate how often you will wear your clothes, you can calculate how much they will cost per day.) You will want something you can wear lots of places and can interchange with your other clothes and accessories.

The well-dressed women of the world are not the ones who

rush out and buy every trendy and faddish garment on the fashion market. On the contrary, the most well-dressed women are the ones who dress "Classic." Classic means stable, never out of style, a lasting impression, good design, and good lines. Classics will be in style for years to come. The hems may go up and down slightly, but the classics are here to stay. (You can even arrive at an unalterable hem length.)

Fun and trendy clothes are okay for an outfit or two but not a whole wardrobe. I would never spend any money of any significance on such an outfit because it's here today and gone tomorrow.

A wonderful friend of mine is the best-dressed woman I know. I have known and met a lot of prominent and wealthy women who have beautiful clothes and look lovely most of the time, but Margarita looks wonderful ALL of the time. She is from Italy and has a natural gift with the basic principles of design.

She is not wealthy, and, by worldly standards, doesn't have a lot of clothes or a great deal of jewelry. She just knows how to put herself together and make every item count. She is a designer and has been involved in the clothing business for years. She has learned how to make the most of any woman's appearance simply by the right apparel. These are some of her most important secrets:

1. Dress only in "your colors."
2. Adhere to body styles.
3. Buy quality. Europeans don't always have a lot of money, and clothes are expensive, but they buy perhaps two outfits a year and alternate them. They buy quality because it lasts and lasts.
4. Dress "classic." This goes hand in hand with buying quality. If you choose styles that will last, buy fabrics and quality that will last, too.

125

5. Be tailored. A woman looks more elegant in clean, crisp lines than lots of fussy prints, frills, and ruffles.
6. Simplicity is the key. Keep outfits simple and clean in line and style. The woman is overdressed who has a hat, shoes, bag, gloves, scarves, jacket, blouse, skirt, pins, bracelets, etc. The more simple you look, the more you show off YOU.
7. Coordinate clothes. Start with a basic wardrobe and add to it as the years go on. If you buy "Classic" and quality, this is easy.
8. Accessorize simply but accessorize. A simple pair of gold earrings, a long chain around the neck, a small pin is enough.
9. Shoes and bag should complement each other. They should never be the main attraction.

Q. What do you mean by classics?

A. A fashion that seems never to go out of fashion. However, there are trends in classics which we must watch for in every season.

Q. What do you mean by trends?

A. Several aspects of clothing are affected by trends:

1. Length of skirts. Select your length according to age and leg shape.
2. Width of lapels. They go from very narrow to very wide. Select the middle width to stay in fashion longer.
3. Shoe shapes. They go from very wide, square toes to very pointed.
4. Shoulder widths vary from natural to padded. Avoid the extremes.
5. Collars vary from small to large. Again, avoid the extremes.

6. For waistlines you are always safe in staying with the natural waistline unless you are selecting a fashion intended to avoid emphasis to your natural waistline.
7. For skirt shapes, the A-line skirt seems never to be out of style. Select a skirt shape that is flattering to your figure.
8. For sleeve shape, stay with the style that looks well on you and watch the current magazines for shapes and lengths that are fashionable.

Q. What is a classic fashion?

A. This is best answered by referring to particular articles of clothing:

1. SHOES
   Patent leather, pump, or sandal with low heel
   Penny loafers or tassel loafers
   Tasseled, leather shoe with low heel
   Leather pump with medium heel and oval toe
   Open-toe sandle shoe with low heel

2. BLOUSES (MOST BLOUSES ARE CLASSICS)
   Shirtwaist
   Button-down, small collar, long sleeves
   Beige or white turtleneck
   Mandarin collar

3. JACKETS AND SWEATERS
   Cowl neck sweater
   Turtleneck sweater
   Blazer
   Cashmere cardigan

4. SKIRTS
   A-line flare
   Pleated in front
   Gathered at waist

5. DRESSES
   Shirtwaist
   Shirtdress
   A-line or flare
   Straight cut with belt

6. PANTS
   Straight line pants

Q. How can I learn to coordinate my wardrobe?

A. Here are a couple of examples:

1. Start with a smart BLAZER in a NEUTRAL COLOR and then select two to four bottoms to go with it to suit your life style (two skirts, one pair of pants, and a dress).
2. Select three tops that will go with all separates (two blouses and one sweater).
3. Select accessories which can be coordinated with the various combinations of wardrobe items (good leather shoes, a good leather handbag [simple design], a belt, if in fashion or needed, a good pin or bracelet, a comb for the hair — look at what the trends are in accessories).

If on the other hand, you started with a black blazer, you might choose a red checked skirt, a gray skirt, black pants for bottoms, and a polka dot dress. For tops you might select a red silk blouse, red sweater, gray blouse, and a white blouse. You will be able to wear any of the tops with any of the bottoms. The one dress is a classic print and can be used with the blazer. The fabric of the blazer could be velveteen or very fine wool.

Q. What are classic prints?

A. Prints that never go out of style — safe purchases.

1. Polka dots
2. Scotch plaids

3. Checks
4. Tweeds
5. Herringbone
6. Paisley
7. Geometric patterns
8. Calico print
9. Stripes

Note: Calico prints are associated with the young look of teens and pre-teens. Strong geometric patterns are associated with sophistication. Therefore, be certain that either of these prints are right for your age and style.

Q. What is the best way to keep up with fashion?

A. Take a monthly fashion magazine that is suitable to your age level. Read it and become familiar with the changes that are taking place. You will always find FADS and CLASSICS in the fashion magazines. It is up to you not to be swayed by FADS if you have a limited budget. There is nothing wrong with buying a FAD if you have the money to spend, and the items look good on you.

We must remember that it takes time to adjust to changes. It is estimated that the average person must see a new trend in fashion for almost three years before they will make the change. If you do not allow your eye to become familiar (through your reading) with the changes, it may be years before you decide to buy something that is practically out of fashion, and your purchase is not going to give you the value you could have received. Another reason to buy classics is that they do not go out of fashion as quickly.

1. Go to local fashion shows.
2. Look in your local dress salons that you know keep better fashions in stock. It doesn't cost anything to shop and

look.

3. Become familiar with designers who are known for their expensive fashions. Watch for the classics they design and try to find copies from other designers who do not charge as much. Look for sales but be careful — you are buying current fashion trends.

Follow the EIGHT CIRCLE PLAN on the following page CAREFULLY WITH ALL OF YOUR BUYS. Know you figure shape, age level, life style, and the best colors for you. You will save many dollars and receive many more compliments on your WARDROBE.

This statement by Sister Barbara B. Smith should also be considered:

> There is wisdom in developing one's sense of style. I once knew a young, attractive buyer in a large department store. She gave a talk to some blind women, at their request, about fashion and style. They had invited her to come to a meeting they held regularly for the purpose of helping them improve their looks.
>
> She sat in that room as the preliminaries were being handled and looked at these well-dressed, sightless women. I don't know what thoughts went through her mind, for she was a woman trained in and sensitive to the visual line and color of ready-made dresses and coats.
>
> But when she stood up and talked, she explained to them the one thing that was the most useful for them to know. I have thought about this many times since, and *I believe it is the most useful single thing for any of us to know about clothes.*
>
> "Fashion," she said, "has to do with fad and

EIGHT POINT FASHION PLAN FOR YOUR WARDROBE

READ . . . OBSERVE . . . LISTEN TO THE EXPERTS

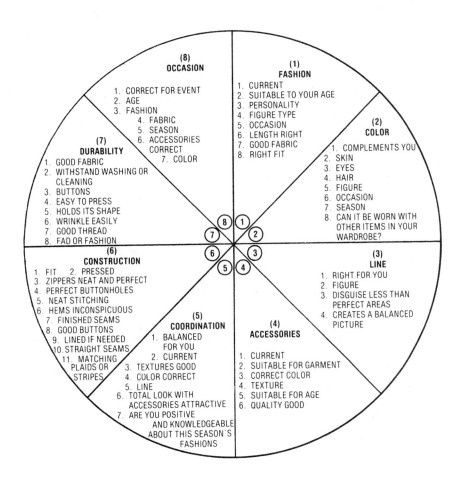

(8) OCCASION
1. CORRECT FOR EVENT
2. AGE
3. FASHION
4. FABRIC
5. SEASON
6. ACCESSORIES CORRECT
7. COLOR

(1) FASHION
1. CURRENT
2. SUITABLE TO YOUR AGE
3. PERSONALITY
4. FIGURE TYPE
5. OCCASION
6. LENGTH RIGHT
7. GOOD FABRIC
8. RIGHT FIT

(7) DURABILITY
1. GOOD FABRIC
2. WITHSTAND WASHING OR CLEANING
3. BUTTONS
4. EASY TO PRESS
5. HOLDS ITS SHAPE
6. WRINKLE EASILY
7. GOOD THREAD
8. FAD OR FASHION

(2) COLOR
1. COMPLEMENTS YOU
2. SKIN
3. EYES
4. HAIR
5. FIGURE
6. OCCASION
7. SEASON
8. CAN IT BE WORN WITH OTHER ITEMS IN YOUR WARDROBE?

(6) CONSTRUCTION
1. FIT   2. PRESSED
3. ZIPPERS NEAT AND PERFECT
4. PERFECT BUTTONHOLES
5. NEAT STITCHING
6. HEMS INCONSPICUOUS
7. FINISHED SEAMS
8. GOOD BUTTONS
9. LINED IF NEEDED
10. STRAIGHT SEAMS
11. MATCHING PLAIDS OR STRIPES

(3) LINE
1. RIGHT FOR YOU
2. FIGURE
3. DISGUISE LESS THAN PERFECT AREAS
4. CREATES A BALANCED PICTURE

(5) COORDINATION
1. BALANCED FOR YOU
2. CURRENT
3. TEXTURES GOOD
4. COLOR CORRECT
5. LINE
6. TOTAL LOOK WITH ACCESSORIES ATTRACTIVE
7. ARE YOU POSITIVE AND KNOWLEDGEABLE ABOUT THIS SEASON'S FASHIONS

(4) ACCESSORIES
1. CURRENT
2. SUITABLE FOR GARMENT
3. CORRECT COLOR
4. TEXTURE
5. SUITABLE FOR AGE
6. QUALITY GOOD

131

style. That which is high fashion is often faddish in nature. It will be good for a short season, and then it will be gone. Style, on the other hand, is the fashion line which is *classic* in nature. It will always be in good taste, with perhaps minor alterations now and then."

So a person can be well dressed by paying close attention to the purchase of a dress with a style that will have a long life and by paying only casual attention to the faddish elements of the new season. (*Blueprints for Living*, vol. 1, p. 40, italics added.)

When buying clothes, buy quality.

For example, about five years ago I bought two suits in my color season: beige and off-white. Each consisted of a skirt and blazer. The fabric was wool gabardine, and they still look new and completely in style. When I purchased them, I could have had three suits for the price of either, but five years later the fabric in a less expensive suit would not have lasted and would probably have lost body and shape. If I divide five years into the amount of money I spent, it turns out that either suit has, by this time, cost me less than even one inexpensive suit.

"So," you are saying, "who wants to wear the same suit every year?" Or maybe you're wondering whether you'll look like everyone else in the same style?

When you buy a lasting garment in quality and style, subsequent purchases are add-ons — items to make the *original purchases interchangeable*. I wear the off-white blazer by itself over dresses for a dressier, formal look, or with jeans and a dressy shirt for a "fun" look. Sometimes I wear the blazer with a cowl neck sweater and wool skirt and boots for a sporty look or with its matching skirt for the suited look.

I wear the off-white skirt to that suit with an off-white cowl neck sweater in the winter for a "winter white" effect. In the warmer months, I wear many different colors of blouses with the skirt and then mix scarves and other accessories for a wide variety of ensembles. Wool gabardine is an all-year fabric suitable for summer and winter. As the years have gone by, I have added other suits, blouses, and pants that are all interchangeable. Any blouse or top which I have can be worked with any skirt, pant, or blazer. All my dresses also coordinate. It's fun to go into my closet and create a whole new outfit that I've never worn before, just from the clothes I have. Yes, I have my favorites that I wear over and over, but when I get tired of them, I just change this blouse, that skirt, etc. Because each item is classic and quality, I can give them a vacation for a year or so, just bring them out again, and it's like having new clothes.

There is another advantage to quality fabrics and styles. They fit beautifully, and you always feel in place. I don't spend a lot of money on clothes. Last year, for example, I didn't buy one new thing, but if the Queen of England came to Las Vegas, I could meet her in style, well groomed, and feeling perfectly at ease about my appearance for the occasion. The style and fit of your clothes should bespeak DIGNITY, CONFIDENCE, AND ELEGANCE (feminine elegance).

Let's talk about everybody looking the same in classic clothes. A woman's colors are her own because they enhance the physical woman. Only you can look like you. Perfect colors and simple lines will flatter that. Clothes should enhance the person, not detract. If all that is seen is the clothes and not the person or the face, those are the wrong clothes.

My nine-year-old daughter, Ashley, drew a picture for me for a lesson I gave in Relief Society. She drew row after row of our ward members seated in a sacrament meeting. I could very easily distinguish who was who by the clothes. There were large, flowering mumus in shocking colors, overwhelming scarves wrapped and wrapped around necks, a handbag bigger than the woman who carried it. The picture was topped off by a pair of feet, protruding from under a pew and adorned with bright red patent leather shoes with huge wooden heels! As my daughter identified each person in the drawing, I saw what she had seen each Sunday — not the person, just the outfit. In the drawing was a woman who dresses very nicely and with dignity. Her characteristics portrayed in my daughter's drawing proved my point. Ashley had drawn her with a big smile and curly hair and wearing a dark, non-descript dress. That's what Ashley had seen and what others saw — the real woman behind those clothes.

Here is the basic classic wardrobe:

1. A tailored suit.   2. A pair of pants that can be coordinated. 3. Three blouses — dressy, tailored, sporty.   4. One turtleneck or cowl neck sweater.   5. Shirtdress with belt.   6. Two pairs of shoes — dressy, sporty.   7. A simple coat.   8. Accessories — scarf, gold chain or strand of pearls, pair of earrings, belt.

This is not a professional model. My sister, Renee McCormick, is a 32-year-old mother of *five* children. Many years ago she too had a weight problem and felt low self-esteem because of it. Today she knows she has gained control of that part of her life. Here she demonstrates the versatility of a few articles of clothing in a basic, classic wardrobe.

To dress classic is in no way limiting. Classic does not mean only tailored lines. There are "romantic" dresses with ruffled necks and full skirts. If you want to interchange with fad looks, you can do that, too. I spend the most money on clothes I wear the most. I always purchase fad clothes on sale.

Time and lack of patience have bleeped out my sewing days, but with needle, thread, and pattern you can create a whole wardrobe with much less money than those who have to purchase theirs. Nevertheless, the same rules about quality apply to you. Why invest all those hours in creating clothes with fifty-cent-a-yard fabric? It used to be that you couldn't get a decently designed dress in a pattern, but I look through those pattern books now and see designers' names roll by like a Paris fashion show. (They would probably literally roll by if they saw their designs being massacred in baby prints and double knit polyester!)

Budget is a great concern of everyone these days. An expensive suit may not be in your budget, and ten-dollar-a-yard fabric seems outrageous, but there is a way! It's called saving money, budgeting money, and shopping sales for clothes or fabric. There are also stores around now that buy up salesmen's samples and overstocked merchandise and are thus able to sell better goods at a discount. In such a store I paid ten dollars for a wool gabardine skirt, fully lined, that would have cost $75 otherwise. I have picked up blouses, sweaters, skirts, and the like for even less than what I could have sewn them for and at a fraction of their original cost.

If you saved $20 a month for one year, that would amount to $240. If you sew, you could make the basic wardrobe with great fabrics — wools and wool blends and fine cottons and rayons. The suit would cost $75, the three blouses would cost $56, pants $20, the dress $40. This adds up to $191. You would then have about $50 to hit the sales for a sweater and two pairs of shoes. (These are estimates based on a size ten pattern and fabric costing between five dollars and ten dollars per yard.) Inflation may destroy these figures but not the principle of planning and budgeting.

A friend of mine asked me to take her shopping. She hadn't bought any new clothes except an occasional dress or two for years. She wore shoes that looked like army boot rejects. She knew she needed to do something but wasn't sure how to do it. She is a large woman with big bones and long arms and legs. Even if she weighed 100 pounds, she would still look like a large woman. She had been colorized and was a winter. She had saved $500 and needed *everything*. After a few stores, this is what she bought (and nothing on sale):

A basic jet black, pure silk shirtdress with long sash
A gray wool gabardine suit (skirt and blazer)
A pair of matching gray wool pants
A pale pair of black wool pants
A gray pin stripped silk blouse
A plum silk blouse
A white silk blouse
A pair of black patent dress sandals
A scarf with wine, plum, black, and white print
A pair of earrings (silver)
A stick pin
Two silver chains
A deep burgundy handbag
A red silk rose
A casual dress
A pair of gray leather pumps

Look at the possibilities in all those interchangeable clothes! She wore the black shirtdress to church with the sash wrapped lightly around her neck and tied with the red rose. Over that she wore the gray blazer. Her gray shoes and burgundy handbag blended in beautifully. She looked tall, thin, graceful, lovely! See how many outfits you can create from her purchases.

It is also important to know how to select accessories that will fit into a planned wardrobe.

Have you ever wondered why there are so many shades of *panty hose* and then just reached for "nude" or "suntan" because they make your legs look so natural. Shades vary and are to be worn with complementary colors.

1. If your clothes are rust, reds, oranges, etc., choose suntan, copper, or russet brown hose.
2. If you are wearing pinks, mauves, plums, wines, etc., choose soft gray, light plum, or mauve hose.
3. If clothes are browns and charcoals, wear brown hose.
4. For tans, camels, taupes, creams, use beige, cream, or taupe hose.
5. For blacks, wear off-black or gray hose.
6. For blues and greens, wear soft gray or beige hose.
7. For pure white or pure cream, wear off-white or cream hose.

As your budget allows, you can wear the darker, opaque colors in the fall and winter and coordinate them with your skirt color. Remember that if you have heavy hips and legs, the total look in skirt or dress and panty hose will take off pounds and give a longer-leg look.

In buying *jewelry*, earrings should be purchased first, then chains and necklaces, a bracelet third, and rings last. Start with earrings because they give you a *finished* look. I have often demonstrated this in a class or seminar by having a woman without earrings come forward and showing those in attendance just how much this simple accessory adds.

Keep your jewelry simple. It is meant to add to the outfit, not detract. Inexpensive, but sensational-looking, costume jewelry makes this addition affordable. One elegant strand of good, imitation pearls will always be a timeless accessory.

Here are some additional pointers:

1. Avoid the earrings that dangle to your shoulders.
2. Never be without earrings, for they add sparkle to the face.
3. Do not wear pins on busy-print fabrics.
4. A few gold chains of varying lengths are much more flattering than a big necklace of gaudy baubles.
5. Choose necklaces that flatter the neckline of the dress or blouse, but do not wear a choker with a high-neck sweater.
6. Bracelets should be coordinated with earrings or necklaces, and earrings should coordinate with necklaces (gold earrings, gold necklace).

Scarves are a fun way to change a basic classic dress from casual to dressy or to add color to your wardrobe. For example, the bodice scarf is great for wearing under a jacket because the scarf looks like a blouse. Here are a few suggestions on how to tie scarves:

WAYS TO FOLD A SCARF

There are three basic ways to fold a scarf —
triangle, bias, and oblong.

WINDSOR KNOT

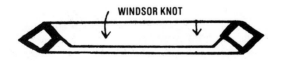

Necktie — Use a large square (at least 31'') folded on the bias; or use an oblong scarf folded narrowly.

143

1. Make the left end shorter than the right.

2. Hold left end with left hand and wind right end around left (2) times.

3. Still holding right end in right hand, pull right end up through the V and down through the loop.

4. Hold left end in left hand and push up knot with right hand.

144

SQUARE KNOT

Use large or small size and follow sketches.

1. Fold into a triangle.

2. Right end over left and tie.

3. Left end over right and tie.

Leave knot in front

Place knot on shoulder

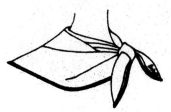

Pony tail

Turban — Using an extra long oblong scarf, wrap around head leaving enough to tie a knot
OR
Place on head and tie knot behind the ear allowing the ends to drape on the shoulder.

Shoes and *handbags* are items most neglected by women everywhere. Here are some good tips:

1. Pay attention to the mood of your outfit. Wear sporty shoes (loafers, low-heeled pumps, tie shoes) with casual clothes or slim, feminine shoes with more delicate heels for dressier clothes.
2. Avoid "clunkers" of any kind. They make your feet look like two lumps of concrete.

3. Build your shoe wardrobe on neutrals to go with your basic season and add colored shoes later.
4. Bright-colored shoes are best only when the color is repeated in another area such as a scarf around the neck.
5. Handbags should also be a neutral — the same color or one shade lighter than your shoes.
6. Avoid handbags that are large with the multi-pockets and compartments that show on the outside, for they make you look clumsy.
7. Try to buy handbags in good leather. A simple, classic leather clutch in your season will last you for years.

With proper planning, saving, and careful shopping you can do it. If all your budget can swing this year is the suit, do it now and then start adding. And while you are saving, you can be getting your body into shape for the new you! However, do not think that because your body is out of shape you can put off good grooming. You must start now to eliminate all that could cause a negative feeling about your appearance. What about clothes you have now that are good either in fabric or quality but aren't in style? RECYCLE them! Here are a few ideas:

1. Big, flared pants from a few years back — cut them off and make them into culottes and wear with knee socks or boots.
2. Small, skimpy jacket — wear it over a sweater and gathered skirt for a Channel look.
3. A tight, slim skirt — wear a large tunic or long, belted sweater over it with dark hose and loafers.
4. Cover that old knit dress with a blazer and then wear boots.
5. Wear a shirt under an old dress and belt it.
6. Cut off that long formal and make it into a mid-calf

length skirt and wear a feminine blouse with it.

7. Remove the bodice of any outdated dress and create a new skirt.
8. Cut off puffy or large sleeves, scoop the neck, and wear over a cowl neck sweater or blouse as a jumper.
9. If your straightline dresses are too short, slit up the side hems and wear as a tunic over pants.
10. Remove the sleeves from an old coat (use them to make a standup collar) and then close the sleeve openings and collar, and you have a stylish cape.

Let me add a word here about dress versus culture. For sisters from Hawaii, Tonga, Japan, or anywhere where the culture or life style may dictate the use of other principles than those discussed here, particular attention should be paid to preserving your great heritage and cultures. I fully believe that tradition should be held in reverence. It is appropriate to wear long, flowering mumus in Hawaii, for example, or beautiful sarongs in India, and so forth. Culture is exciting. In any case, the apparel should be authentic and native to the area.

TIPS FOR SHOPPING SALES

There is an art to shopping sales. Large sales in department stores are geared to impulse buying. Often you buy something because you see it on "sale" and probably not because you really need it. I used to come home from sales with a blouse that didn't go with anything I had or a dress that was the wrong color or a pair of shoes that I didn't find out were uncomfortable until I got home.

The first thing to understand in learning to shop sales is what a REAL sale is. If you look at a price tag and see a *printed* price that has been marked over with an ink pen in someone's writing, that item is REALLY on sale. Part of merchandising is the creation of sales. In other words, if you look at a price tag and see the *printed* price in black, marked out by a *printed* red line, and the "sale" price *printed* in red, that item has been brought in by the store as "sale merchandise." Usually you are paying the regular (profit) price for these items. Lately, I have seen small *printed* tapes on top of the printed price tag. These items are also real sales. The tapes were prepared at another location and affixed to the regular price tag.

Knowing these things, here are some rules for shopping sales:

1. Don't go to a sale if you don't need anything.
2. If you need a pair of shoes, shop only for shoes and stick to your plan.
3. Buy only in your season (autumn, spring, summer, winter).
4. Buy only an item that can be worn or coordinated with something else you own.
5. Carry swatches of fabric if you sew, from your clothes, to match in the store.
6. Don't buy something that's a DOG, which is probably on sale because the store can't get rid of it because of its ugly color, ill fit, poor quality, too many of them, etc. Be careful. Be discriminating.

BODY SHAPES

Buy, borrow, or rent a leotard and tights, put them on and stand in front of a full-length mirror. Have a friend help you in determining your body structure. There are six basic body types:

1. Triangular — narrow shoulders and wide hips.
2. Inverted triangular — wider upper torso and slim hips and legs.
3. Square — short waist, hip and shoulder area the same.
4. Tall and slim — over 5'8" and under 130 pounds.

5. Petite — under 5'3".
6. Ideal — 5'6" to 5'8", legs and torso well proportioned.

Triangular Figure

Figure with narrow shoulders and wide hips:
DO:
1. Give width through the shoulders, bust, and upper arms.
2. Detract attention from hips with line and color.
3. Wear solid, dark colors over hips.
4. Wear styles with a flare or pleat continuing from hipline. Full skirts are ideal for formal length dresses.
5. Stress shoulder and neckline interest with collars and jewelry.
6. Use sleeves with fullness at the shoulder to broaden upper torso.
7. Wear boleros and short jackets that end above or at the waist. Also wear full, hem length coats.
8. Use pastels and bright colors above the waist to draw attention from the hips.
9. Carry handbags (not too wide), gloves, and shoes to match your skirt in color. Be sure these accessories are proportioned to your height.
10. If tall enough, wear hats with width and height. If shorter, be sure hat is as wide as widest part of face.
11. Use vertical or diagonal lines in skirt detail. Button skirt or side draping.
12. Wear necklaces and earrings. Don't center pins.
13. Coats should be semi-fitted or designed in straight, loose fitting lines. Never belt.
14. Self-fabric belts and narrower ones.

DON'T:
1. Never wear sleeves with fullness or cuffs at hip level.
2. Never wear unmounted or raglan sleeves to narrow the shoulders.
3. Long jackets and ¾ length coats give width to hips — avoid this.
4. Avoid fleecy, heavy fabrics and light colors at hips.
5. Avoid "cinch" belts and wide belts that cause the hips to push out below the waist.
6. Never tightly-fitted skirts. Soft ease in the skirt is more flattering.

Do

Don't

Inverted Triangular Figure
Figure with a wider upper torso and slim hips and legs:

DO:

1. Slenderize the upper torso and attract attention to hips and legs.
2. Wear hats with an upward tilt brim. Profile hats are good. Be sure the hat is as wide as the widest part of the face, wider if your height permits.
3. Wear lines and styles that add length to the upper torso. Vertical stripes and pleats are good.
4. Low necklines are good for you. If it is off shoulder or strapless, be certain it doesn't fit too snug, or there will be bulges.
5. If upper arms are heavy, keep them covered with narrow sleeves.
6. Do use padding in shoulders so their width equals bust width. Clever designs can do this.
7. Your skirt is best with a slight hemline flare, even though your hips are slim. A tight or narrow skirt accents the upper body weight.
8. Checks, plaids, and light colors may be used for skirt's fabric but not for blouse and jacket.
9. Wear straight line jackets and coats without large collars. Tuxedo style is good.
10. Wear semi-fitted princess lines.
11. Accessories should be in keeping with your height. Contrasting gloves or a purse are good as attention is drawn to the hip area.
12. Large bracelets and earrings may be worn but not heavy necklaces.

DON'T:

1. Too small hat or hats with a turned down effect.
2. Wear large collars or large necklines.

3. Sweaters that fit snugly. Choose softly draped bodice styles.
4. Avoid severely tailored bodices and jackets.
5. Dolman and bat winged sleeves add width to torso.
6. Unusual belts and contrasting colors which match skirt or top.
7. Heavy necklaces.

Do

Don't

Square Figure
Figure with short waist, hip and shoulder area same: good lines for overweight figure.

DO:

1. Vertical and diagonal lines add to height and slenderize.
2. One-piece dresses are more flattering than suits as less bulk around hip area.
3. Semi-fitted, flared skirt is ideal. One-piece dress should be single breasted with no belt.
4. Vertical and diagonal button closings. Stripes are good.
5. Wear short (just above the elbow) and waist length narrow sleeves.
6. Simple, collarless necklines that are high or low are best for you.
7. Hats should have a decided upward tilt. Width same as widest point of face. Wider if height permits.
8. Coats should be full length and straight lines.
9. Handbags should match costume color but large enough to minimize your figure.
10. Wear gloves that match your costume color. Avoid whites and pastels.
11. Wear skirts a fraction longer than fashion dictates.

DON'T:

1. Wear printed, checked, or plaid fabrics.
2. Avoid pastels, heavy, or shiny fabrics. Trim on cuff or necklines is all right.
3. Avoid jersey, knits, satins, and any fabric that clings to the figure. If the fabric is fully lined and made to not cling, then can wear.
4. Do not wear skirt, blouse, or sweater combinations (matched okay).
5. Sleeveless or cap sleeves unless arms are slender.

6. Avoid capes, boleros, ruffles, bows, or fussy trims.
7. Avoid sandals or flat heeled shoes.
8. Keep jewelry in one area and sized to your height.
9. Tucked in blouses and tight belts.
10. Very full gathered skirts.

Do

Don't

The Tall, Slim Figure

DO:

1. Use horizontal and curved lines to your advantage.
2. If you are well proportioned, vertical and diagonal lines create a dramatic effect by accenting your height.
3. Wear massive jewelry (rings, bracelets, necklaces, unusual and large handbags, high fashion gloves in contrasting color if desired).
4. Wear medium and large size hats. Wear turned down brims to cut inches. Wear bright colored hats. Be sure hat is as wide as widest part of face. Give thought to shape of face and line of hat.
5. Wear full sleeves, dolman, wide cuffs, ¾ length sleeves, and long gloves with short or strapless dresses.
6. Wear wide collars, contrasting scarves, choker necklaces, and draped necklines.
7. An accented long-waisted appearance cuts leg length.
8. Tunics, peplums, long suit jackets, ¾ length coats, and dropped waistlines.
9. Wear gathered, pleated, tiered, and flared skirts and eased sheaths.
10. Wide sashes and belts in contrasting colors.
11. When wearing straight line skirts or dresses, cut the vertical effect by a longer jacket, wide belt, hip pockets, or pegged skirt. Keep horizontal lines in a stitching, etc.
12. Wear simple shoes with a short vamp. These may contrast.
13. Wear plaids, checks, and prints unless overweight.
14. Wear bulky, loose fitting coats belted styles or ¾ length.
15. Capes are becoming if waist length or longer.
16. A slim sheath should not fit too tightly.
17. Knits and bulky fabrics are good.
18. Long haired fur jackets, scarves, and muffs are becoming.
19. Separates are ideal for the tall girl.

DON'T:
1. Avoid small pieces of jewelry and small handbags.
2. Do not wear vertical lines in hats or feathers up.
3. Boleros and vestees must be teamed with full skirts.
4. Avoid vertical rows of buttons and trims (unless full figure).
5. Small furs.
6. Avoid too many points of interest. Makes you look massive.

Do

Don't

Petite Figure

Under 5'3" is considered petite. A good rule to follow is dress tall if you are 5'5" or under.

DO:

1. Dress in an extremely simple fashion to create a vertical line.
2. Jewelry will be smaller as well as handbags.
3. Whenever possible, don't break the line of color. Dressing monochromatically gives a taller appearance. Keep attention at the top of your costume.
4. Wear a V cut vamp shoe. Pumps are better than sandals. Wear as high a heel as is in fashion. Be comfortable.
5. Wear sleeveless dresses or long, slim sleeves. Avoid different color cuffs and big, puffy sleeves.
6. Choose dresses, coats, and suits with a vertical line. Princess, A-line, and shift lines are very good.
7. Boleros and brief capes are good. Suit jackets are best not more than 4 to 6 inches below the waist.
8. Wear skirts a bit longer than currently in fashion. Long skirts will make you appear taller.
9. Wear skirt and blouse in matching tones.
10. Full length coats, fitted or straight lines.
11. Wear high, small collars and plain necklines with small yolk details suitable to face shape. Wear smaller prints and patterns.
12. Wear costume detail and jewelry at shoulder and upper bodice.
13. Hats should have an upward line.

DON'T:

1. Overdress.
2. Three-quarter length sleeves, wide cuffs, and full sleeves.
3. Tunics, peplums, wide belted jackets, long jackets, and different colored belts.

4. Avoid any skirt detail except vertical line buttons or trim.
5. Do not wear two color costumes or large prints.
6. Avoid large collars and heavy scarves. Keep them smaller.
7. Massive jewelry and choker necklaces that are large. Limit jewelry interest at top of dress. Waist length cuts height.
8. Contrasting belts and wide belts.
9. Large hats and bags are not for you.
    Be proud of being small and slim.

 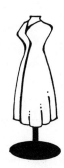 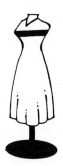 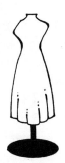

Do

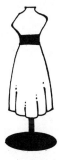  

Don't

The Ideal Figure

5'6" to 5'7" is considered the ideal figure if weight is correct. Your bone structure will determine line of clothes best for you.

DO:

1. Remember you can wear almost any design. It will depend on what line you wish to create.
2. The vertical line attracts more attention to you. It expresses dignity and importance.
3. The horizontal line will cut your height. It shows relaxation and repose.
4. Diagonal lines will give you movement and show aggressiveness. They can be very dramatic and often exciting in design.
5. Curved lines express gracefulness, femininity and are very beautiful with certain fabrics.
6. Let your accessories be judged by your bone structure. If you are larger boned, you can wear bolder and larger jewelry.
7. Your wardrobe should express your personality and moods.
8. Remember to watch carefully where a jacket hits you at the hip level, especially if it is a different color. You can wear jackets well, but if you are inclined to be hippy, this will exaggerate them.
9. Simplicity will always be your best rule. Don't wear too many points of interest.
10. Observe new fashion trends in accessories, etc.
11. Play up your best points.
12. Keep your hats as wide as the widest part of your face or more.

DON'T:

1. Overdress. (Jot down other ideas.)

After you determine your basic body shape, stand against a door and have your friend mark with a pencil your height, leg length at thigh joint, then your waist, armpit, and finally your knee joint. Stand back and analyze whether or not you are long waisted, short waisted, long armed, and short or long legged for your total body height. The average leg length is half of your entire height. The waist should fall between armpit and leg height. Elbows should be at the waist.

Decide what your flaws and pluses are and then use the following guides to help you avoid clothes and lines that will accentuate the negative. These guides are also intended to help you in focusing on the positive.

1. NECK
   Too Long:
   - Avoid short hair.
   - Avoid deep V necklines.
   - Wear scarves, chokers, ribbons.
   - Wear collars and cowl necklines.

   Too Short:
   - Wear open collar, V, or scoop neck.
   - Avoid high collars or turtlenecks.
   - Short hair is better.

   Too Wide:
   - Wear a crew neckline close to the base of the neck (front and back).

2. ARMS
   Too Long:
   - Wear wide cuffs (especially in contrasting colors).
   - No three-quarter length sleeves.
   - Short sleeves should hit one inch above or below bust, not at bust.

Too Short:
  •Wear long sleeves.
  •Wear three-quarter length sleeves.
  •No cuffs or ruffles.

Too Heavy:
  •No tight-fitting long sleeves as they accent bulges.

3. BUST
  Too Large:
    •*Do not* wear tight-fitting blouses.
    •Avoid sleeve lengths that hit at bust.
    •Avoid horizontal lines at bust level.
    •Avoid high-waisted look.
    •Avoid belts.
    •Wear collars open.

  Too Small:
    •Wear blouses with fullness.

4. WAIST
  Very Small:
    •If with large bust and hips, avoid a "nipped" in the middle look.

  Wide:
    •Avoid belts.
    •Use the "no waist" look by a blouson top.

  Too Short:
    •Avoid belts.
    •Darker colors should be worn above waist.

  Too Long:
    •Use wide belts.
    •Darker colors should be worn below the waist.

5. HIPS
   Too Narrow:
   - Hip pockets are good on pants.
   - Wear full and gathered skirts.

   Too Wide:
   - No pockets or fullness at hip line.
   - No A-line skirts.
   - Gentle gathering at the waist is ideal.
   - Always have slight fullness in a skirt or dress.
   - Avoid cinching your waist.
   - Loose vests are good.

6. LEGS
   Short:
   - No cuffs on pants.
   - Wear high heels.
   - Keep suit jackets no longer than crotch.
   - Wear short blouses.

   Long:
   - Avoid high-waisted styles in pants, skirts, dresses.
   - Wear tunics.

MATERNITY FASHIONS

Of all the times a woman should look her absolute best (and probably feels her worst), the most important time is when she is pregnant. This is a time when you feel so much like "letting go" because you've lost your figure, and you feel the fatigue of pregnancy. But I promise you that if you will try to be especially attractive at this time in your life, you *will* feel more confident and positive about your appearance.

Make-up, hair, colors, are all factors, but the biggest mistake pregnant women make is in their clothing. During my last pregnancy I went shopping for a whole new wardrobe and hours and hours later came home with one dress. With the pregnancies of all my friends and relatives, I have searched the stores for good maternity fashions. They are far and few between!

There are horrible tee shirts with undignified verses on them or arrows pointing to the belly, little baby doll frocks and dress, and the worst I've seen yet was the dress with a giant watermelon on the belly!

It seems as if most maternity designers are trying to poke fun at a most sacred time of a woman's life. Either that or they're just trying to "make it big enough to shove it all under there!"

These are some tips that will help you dress with dignity during pregnancy:

Wear clothes or tops gathered at the *shoulders*. The same principle applies here as applies to someone with wide hips. The fullness should ease over the body. As you can see, gathering above or below the bust accentuates the middle.

Don't   *Do*

Never wear tops that end at the hip. Lengthen them to at least the knee or slightly above, and you will see a smaller figure instantly.

Do

Don't

When wearing dresses, keep stockings and shoes close to natural skin tones (neutrals) for a longer-leg look.

Scarves around the neck focus on the neck and face and take away from the middle area.

Jewelry should be simple and kept close to the face. Never let it hit over the belly.

Wear solid colors as much as possible and keep prints small. Avoid large, busy prints.

Don't

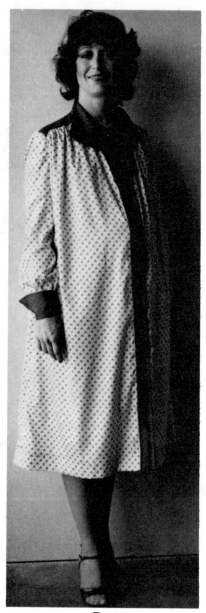

Do   *Do*

Avoid stiff fabrics. Soft, draping ones are more flattering.

Do

Do NOT wear clothes that are too tight.

Don't

THE BUSINESS WOMAN

As a business woman, there is a certain image to maintain. It is one of confidence, poise, and decisiveness. It is an image that is representative of the association of the individual with the firm. It is such an image that is characteristic of the Prophet, the General Authorities, and full-time missionaries. Even their appearance must be representative of the association which they have with the Lord. They are His emissaries. The guidelines that apply to their good image are the same that should apply to you as member missionary, daughter of God, homemaker, and woman.

Summarizing what this chapter has outlined, here is an overall view of how you may project a better outward image. By doing so your self-confidence and self-esteem will immediately increase.

Here is Renee again wearing clothes that demonstrate poor design, unflattering line, distracting pattern, and an overall unfeminine look:

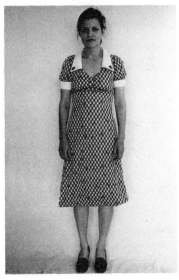

Babyish or childish print and style   Poor design, unfeminine fabric

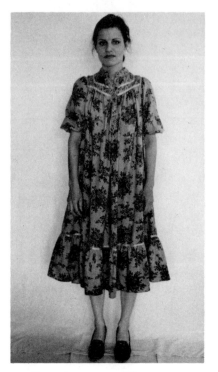

Unflattering cut and line.

Distracting print. Long dresses for daytime are unstylish.

Here is Joann Evans, our secretary, the wife of a bishop, mother of seven children, and by the date of this book's release, a grandmother:

Bulky handbag
Matronly blouse
Frumpy appearance
Cut of jacket is unflattering

Excellent print
Classic line
Small handbag
Feminine shoes

Classic line
Excellent print
Youthful feeling

A GOOD IMAGE

Hair/Make-up/Glasses

Hair should always be sparkling clean. Stay away from fluffy, overdone, or too severe hair styles. Hair should not fall below your shoulders.

Wear make-up. Be sure it is applied correctly for a finished appearance. It should not be too heavy or too bright. Colors should blend in with skin tone and eye color, as explained in the section on color analysis.

Do not wear colored lenses. No one will be able to look you in the eye. Eyeglass frames should be simple.

Body Language

Keep your head up to show you are in control and able to look others in the eye. Walk with grace and purpose and keep your walk smooth and even instead of slinking or shuffling.

Stay fit. Keep your body as trim as possible. Hold your hands in front of you when standing or talking, develop a firm handshake to avoid appearing timid or shy, and learn how to enunciate your words and speak with assurance and vitality.

Fashion

Wear simple, classic outfits and avoid wild prints and flashy fabrics. Clothes should not be too complicated or confusing. Dresses, suits, skirts, and blouses are your best bet.

Darker colors indicate that you are a decision maker. However, this does not mean you have to look dull and uninteresting. Combine scarves and jewelry to brighten up an outfit and wear a rich-colored, polyester, silk, or Crepe de chine blouse to soften a conservative suit.

Simple gold chains or a string of pearls and pearl earrings are always in good taste. Stay away from an abundance of rings and noisy bracelets.

Handbags and shoes should be of good quality. Carry a small classic clutch. Keep your handbags neat and not overstuffed, and polish and repair your shoes regularly.

Putting it all together — personal hygiene, weight control, fitness, good health, make-up, hair, and clothes — is not an art developed overnight. Do not be discouraged if you don't seem to slide right into a new image. It will take effort, studying, and practice, but remember that one of the few things that never go out of style is a feminine woman.

Do not be concerned about the cost of a new image. I am not in favor of anyone spending great amounts of money on clothing or beauty care. You shouldn't jeopardize your monthly budget in pursuit of clothes and glamour, but with common sense and careful planning, you can take all the ideas outlined in this chapter and apply them to your personal economy. Whether you sew, recycle, or purchase, the same amount of time, energy, and money usually goes equally into a poor choice or a good choice. Learn to choose correctly.

What makes a woman beautiful? It is chastity, charity, sacrifice, endurance, and self-acceptance — a role and an *image* that began in the household of God.

Part Two

Chapter  Five

A House of Order

"Organize yourselves; prepare every needful thing; and establish a house, even a house of prayer, a house of fasting, a house of faith, a house of learning, a house of glory, a house of order, a house of God . . . . Cease to be idle; cease to be unclean . . ."
—Doctrine and Covenants 88:119, 124

As a professional interior designer for over ten years, I have come to understand that the structure in which a family lives (the family's physical environment) is almost as important in becoming a celestial family as the attitudes of the family's members.

What is a celestial home? For a long time I looked at the idea of home as somehow being the personality of the people in the home and their attitude towards one another. However, the people or the *family* cannot become a *home*; they become a celestial family. In other words, the attitude towards celestial family life cannot be nurtured without the environment of a celestial home — the building or structure in which the family lives. Three things are essential in making a structure or house into a celestial home: cleanliness, privacy, and personality.

People interpret their homes in so many different ways because of personality, tastes (whether they be good or bad), and money.

Attention to these three things will make it easier for you to invite the spirit of the Lord to dwell with you in your home. The physical environment of the family is directly related to its spiritual well-being.

Whenever I go to the temple I know that I am in a celestial home, for it is clean, private, and reflects the dignity of Him whose house it is. The following thoughts can be extended to include our physical surroundings:

> You want to live so that your minds will be filled with his Spirit; and to do this, you need not take a mission to the sun, to the moon, or to the stars, to find out their distances or how much they weigh. But are you acquainted with your home? You answer, 'Yes.' Well, then, do right at home, do not do wrong, do not quarrel at home, do not stir up disunion, do not, in a word, do anything to bring about a pandemonium instead of a paradise; but do that which brings peace — that which produces the spirit of peace and of heaven.
>
> But where . . . discord exist(s), the principles of heaven are not there; the principles of peace are not there. Study these principles, and for what purpose? Why, that it may stir up the spirit of peace within you — that the spirit of peace may be, not a casual visitor, but a constant attendant — that he may take up his abode with you; and when an individual takes up his

abode with you, then you do not consider him a transient visitor, but there is his home— there is where he lodges, where he stays, where he imparts blessings — where he imparts good. . .

And if you open a door that this Spirit will take up his abode with you, then that fountain which will be opened up will become very plenteous in its supplies; it will become so to you because you welcome the Holy Spirit there, and you study to cultivate within you such a feeling that the Spirit will love to tarry with you. . ."

Journal of Discourses 5:310

You've been taught how desirable it is to have the Spirit with you, yet He cannot abide with you if you are unclean in person as well as in thought and deed. He cannot abide with you if you are unorganized and undisciplined. The same holds true for your home. The Spirit cannot come and live where it is dirty, unorganized, and undisciplined; and if the Spirit is not within the structure, as in the temple, it's very difficult to keep it with the members of the family. It's almost next to impossible to have a celestial family without a celestial home.

About three years ago we decided to build a new home. We put our old one up for sale and began construction. It was at the time that the interest rates were climbing overnight, and people were nervous. We had a lot of equity in our home, and it meant the new buyers would either have to refinance or give us a huge amount of cash. With the precarious interest rates, the market was soft, and no one was buying, and very few people had cash. We put our house up for sale early, thinking it might take the entire six months of construction time or longer to sell it. Very unexpectedly a buyer showed up with cash! We quickly went out and leased a home for six months and put all of our belongings into storage except our clothes, kitchen items, and a little furniture. For six months we felt completely disoriented, but we survived. It was a clean home, and we kept it clean. We continued with our routines and "pretended" that we were home. Six months passed, the lease expired, and our new home was still a few weeks away from completion, as severe winds and bad weather had slowed up the construction. The landlord would only sign six month leases, so we moved into my sister's living room! (They, too, were building next door to us.) Their house was finished first, and a week later they moved, leaving us behind in their home (which they had just rented out). The renters were about to move in behind us. Our house still wasn't ready, but we made the decision to move in anyway. One toilet was hooked up, and we had one sink — in opposite bathrooms — kitchen sink, no appliances or countertop. We only had concrete floors, and we did our cooking on a Coleman camp stove. (Oh, I thought, if my clients could see me now!) A few days later, my other sister, who was building on the opposite side of us, came over and said that their house had also been cashed out. They needed to move immediately, and their new house didn't even have the power on yet. So, in they came: sister, husband, and five children. It was pandemonium!

Within a few weeks, everything was beginning to settle down. They got the power turned on and moved in. We got the plumbing and the kitchen finished and at least the main rooms carpeted. But then, when the dust began to settle and the weeks went by, I noticed a difference in our family. Nothing seemed to go right. We were bickering constantly, accidents seemed to happen easier, and everyone was on edge. Steve and I didn't even have our usual "can't wait to see you" attitude. There was no spirit of peace or harmony in our home.

Slowly I began to realize what had happened. We had come

from a clean, well-kept, attractive home. For over half a year we had been "camping," and even though we were in our new home, it wasn't organized and consequently, neither were we. We had been hit-and-miss with family prayers, personal interviews, family home evening, and we just weren't providing an environment that would invite the spirit of the Lord. We had grieved the Spirit. I remembered this statement by the Apostle Paul: "And grieve not the Holy Spirit of God, whereby ye are sealed unto the day of redemption. Let all bitterness, and wrath, and anger, and clamour, and evil speaking, be put away from you" (Ephesians 4:30-31).

We had been living in "clamour" and confusion, and we had allowed ourselves to become governed by our environment instead of controlling it. As we let the environment rule us, we had neglected to put the matters of the family first. When the affairs of the family had taken second place, we had grieved the Spirit, and things had not gone right. Steve and I held an emergency meeting and then a family council. Within twenty-four hours we were back on course. We organized ourselves, listed priorities, and started to work. First, we got the kitchen in order, then the children's bedrooms, and instead of landscaping, we spent the money to finish the window coverings, floor coverings, and all the other small adjustments that would give our home a finished feeling. We made the living room a place where we could congregate and talk and be together in cleanliness, peace, and privacy.

Of course, our situation was extreme and peculiar, but the point is the same. A disorganized and an unclean home, one that has a "thrown together" or maybe I should say "throw it at me" look, IS EXTREME, and the spirit of the Lord will not dwell there. You know that you want a celestial family, don't you want a celestial home? Sure you do! Your home doesn't have to be featured on the cover of *House Beautiful* in order to be pleasing, comfortable, and celestial!

Throughout that whole experience I learned an important concept about being a woman, wife, mother, and homemaker. When the Spirit was gone, when I procrastinated, I felt lousy about myself. My personal inefficiency made me feel guilty, nervous, and on edge. I knew I contributed a great deal to my family's discord.

No matter what your home is like — a trailer, cabin, apartment, tract home, custom home, or a mansion — your first responsibility is to keep it clean and organized. There are some direct benefits resulting from a clean home:

1. You are free from the guilt of knowing that it is dirty. Everytime you pass the storage closet overloaded with debris or walk over a dirty floor or brush your teeth in front of a sticky mirror, it echoes that you just keep pushing it aside. It is that haunting guilt that stays with you. It is easier for me to be mentally free to accomplish all I want to do when I get down on hands and knees, scrub the floor, and get that out of the way of my thoughts.

2. Your family is learning good techniques and skills from you. If you live in dirt and clutter, you are daily teaching your family that that is acceptable behavior. Your daughters will grow up and be the same kind of house-keepers, and your sons will create problems for their wives. And what will their children be like? You are rearing generations of people who don't respect either self or home! However, if your home is clean and orderly, you need the cooperation of the whole family to keep it that way. Hence, you are teaching them care, concern, and respect. Generations will follow you and rise up and call you blessed for the example of pride and

self-respect which you instilled in the hearts of your posterity.

3. You develop pride in your home and in yourself. In other words, your home is a statement about how you feel about yourself. I am not speaking of pride and vanity but self-esteem. You love your home when it is clean; you are glad to be there. You want to care for it and express yourself there. It is a place to exhibit and explore your talents.

4. Others can enjoy your home more. A client came to me once and said that she needed new carpet or wallpaper in her home, something to cheer it up. She said her children's friends and her neighbors made excuses for not coming over. When I went there to see the home, I didn't even have to go inside to know why no one wanted to enter. As she opened the door, a rancid odor of grease, cooked foods, and body odors rushed out the door almost overwhelming me! Here was a woman who could afford a few luxuries, yet she hadn't tackled the problem of caring for the home and the possessions which she had. As I walked through the house, I saw old banana peels in the corner of one room, crusty window sills, counters stained with all types of things, a stove and backsplash so greasy that the dust stuck to it, bathroom tiles lined with black, "living" matter that you could have grown things in, draperies dragging with dust, and furniture that was soiled and gray. I wanted to leave. No, I wanted to run! As she talked about the new this and the new that which she wanted, I hardly heard a word she said. I was getting a headache from the combination of the odors and whether I should or shouldn't level with this woman.

Finally, I didn't care if I lost the job. This woman

needed help, and she really wanted others to enjoy her home. As we talked, I told her of my impression, even as her front door had opened. We walked from room to room and talked about each disaster area. She was nervous, twitched, and got teary eyed. I asked her what difference she thought it would make if she were to buy new things only to have them end up like this?

We wrote down a plan.

Weeks later she called, and I went back to her house. As the door opened, a fresh, pine smell rushed past me. As we walked from room to room, I noticed that the crust was gone, the grease and "living" things had disappeared, walls were washed or painted, clean sheets hung at some windows where there had been ragged draperies, and the rugs and furniture had been shampooed. She was ready to start redecorating — reliving. The house was ready for new possessions, which would be KEPT new and fresh and clean.

In the spirit of the missionary effort, your home needs to be a place where others will appreciate your example. Your home must be a place where the gospel can be taught (whether by precept or by example), as well as a place of refuge to those who need the love of the gospel in their lives. A clean, orderly home makes a welcome environment for the gospel in others' lives.

5. The Savior can come to your home anytime for you are ready for Him. Do you actually realize that we belong to the Lord? Everything we have is His? He has given us the stewardship of caring for, respecting, and honoring that which is His. How you care for His home is something for which you will one day give an account. He has said this of his own house: "Behold, mine house is a house of order, saith the Lord God, and not a house of confus-

sion" (D&C 132:8).

I want Him to know that His house on Patrick Lane in Las Vegas is in order and ready for Him. Don't you feel that way about your home?

When the Lord said, "Let all things be done in cleanliness before me" (D&C 42:42), He meant ALL things.

How, then, do you go about getting a home clean and orderly and keeping it that way?

There have been quite a few books published through Latter-day Saint publishers on home management and organization. Two by Darryl Hoole, *The Joy of Homemaking* and *The Art of Homemaking*, are well worth reading.

The first thing you must do is have a plan. In that plan you must: (1) list priorities, (2) have a schedule, and (3) chart out that schedule and then ACT.

When a friend of mine was in a Relief Society presidency in Utah, she and the other members of the presidency were greatly concerned over the ungodlike living conditions of many of the sisters in their ward. They put their hearts and heads together and came up with the idea of forming a group called "Householics." I was so impressed with the idea and its success that I asked her to write the experience down:

> In our ward there were some sweet gals who were feeling overwhelmed as mothers, home-makers, etc. They felt they weren't keeping abreast of their everyday routines.
>
> We knew we had to teach the sisters the skills and the principles they had left behind. We didn't want to just go in and take over because they would have missed the point. A working plan was devised that would *teach* the women basic housekeeping skills. We needed to make it

189

basic enough for the beginner and broad enough for the sisters who wanted to improve on their skills. We were very prayerful and consulted the Lord daily to help us pull it together. How could we get the women involved, how could we get them to come? How could we involve the sisters who really needed it without offending them? These questions (and a lot of others throughout the program) we would ask as a presidency. We would ask, and the Lord would answer. How to get them interested was the first question. We presented this marvelously funny skit at Relief Society. One sister was laden with dirty dishes, dirty clothes, and dirty children. She entered the room moaning and groaning, clanging and banging as she spewed out all the excuses for her untidy home. Before she knew what hit her, in bolted another sister wearing a red cape and the letters "SH" (Super Housekeeper) appliqued on her shirt. With a lot of funny lines, some horrible puns, and a few references about the Board of Health, we knew we had started with a bang!

The program ran every other week for six weeks. It was only one hour long. We allowed thirty minutes for the lesson and thirty minutes for discussion. We then proposed that everyone choose a buddy. The purpose of the buddy, of course, was for us to help each other reach our goals. We set *one* goal a week, and then would set up a time *each day* to call our buddy for a report. We talked about the basic problems and tried to come up with the formula to make it work for us. We got some information for our lessons from homemaking books and tapes on the subject. We'd put the lesson together and then relied on the spirit to present it. We had guest speakers who had both large and small families.

Our guests included Utah Young Mother of the Year, Utah Family of the Year, and some sisters from our own ward who had been the route. It was very good for us to know we weren't alone in our feelings. We talked about small quarters with no storage space and gave ideas. We talked about how to decorate on a shoe-string budget, how to retrain a husband, and how to retrain children. Once we had a cosmetic expert come and give us a demonstration. We talked about what styles looked good on whom, how to buy, what to make, buying the right fabrics, etc. We also discussed ideas for children's rooms, the kitchen, and other rooms. After we had taught the sisters how to keep their homes, they felt better about themselves. They started asking about how to wallpaper, paint, and make curtains. We decided to have a workshop. We talked it over with our bishop, and he agreed we could wallpaper the kitchen in the meetinghouse.

We organized a work crew. The women cleaned the entire kitchen. They washed walls, vacuumed drawers, scrubbed floors, cleaned the refrigerator and oven. A wonderful thing had happened: they were using the skills they had learned and could see the end result.

The wallpapering part was fun! Everyone got a turn, either with pasting, cutting, measuring the wall, rolling the seams, or trimming. All in all, they saw it started and finished. With dirt under our nails and wallpaper paste in our hair, we marked our first success. The kitchen was a delight to work in. In the weeks that followed, everyone who used it loved it and wanted to keep it immaculate. The same thing was true for the sisters who had jazzed up their own kitchens and homes.

They felt good about themselves and felt they *could* keep up. They had also made a real friend, for the buddy they had chosen several weeks before had become a real sister.

One sister noted that when she went up to make her bed, her children did, too. As she kept the living room tidy, the children did the same in their rooms. One sister's husband even got the bug. He washed, waxed, and vacuumed out the car. Another sister lost twenty-five pounds and became more aware of her appearance. Some of the other sisters found that they even had extra time on their hands. With this extra time, one gal took up cake decorating and helped supplement the family income. They found that they had time for scripture study, and we saw a growth in their spirituality.

There were many such successes, and we were grateful that we had heeded the promptings of the Spirit. I am grateful for the three women in that presidency, for their unselfish love, for the women they had stewardship over, and for my "buddy" who loved me and helped me achieve my goals.

This is the outline of the program:

Week 1 **What's the Problem?**
- Let sisters talk about individual problems
- Pick a buddy
- Set goals
- Encourage

Week 2 **ABC's of Housekeeping**
- Some practical solutions (washing dishes as soon as meals are over, making the bed as soon as you get up, etc.)
- Set a schedule (time limit) to have basic housework done

Week 3 **Donate to Deseret Industries**
- Clean out cabinets
- Children's clothes (too small, etc.)
- Throw away duplicates
- Bag, box, etc., unwanted items

Week 4 **Turning Over A New Leaf**
- Set some house rules (no eating in the living room, everyone makes own bed, etc.)
- Assign older children to help little ones
- Assign jobs to individuals (setting table, trash, clearing table, drying dishes, etc.)

Week 5 **Storage Space (Rearrange or Recreate)**
- Kids' rooms
- Toys
- Food
- Garage

Week 6   Feminine or Frump
- •Be good to yourself
- •Choosing clothes (mini fashion show, workshop, etc.)
- •Cosmetics (demonstration, workshop, etc.)
- •Hair styles and hair care
- •Good diet

For the workshops the sisters listened to each other's ideas and came up with a list of things they wanted to learn. Here are a few of their ideas:

Childrens' Rooms:
   How to make:
      Toy Box
      Shelves
      Toy Tree
      Toy Bags
      Curtains (using sheets)

Other Rooms:
   How to wallpaper
   How to paint
   Upholstering furniture
   Refinishing furniture
   Jazzing up a room with accessories

Personal Care:
   Fashion show
   Quick tips on applying make-up

Couldn't you just feel the spirit and comraderie of these spirits as my friend talked of their service and sharing? Their program, of course, was tailored to their ward members' needs. Such a program for your area would perhaps focus on different aspects of home clean up.

Sister Cindy Cook of Menan, Idaho, has given me permission to share this Work File System with you:

WORK FILE

Take Saturday and Sunday off. Work Monday through Friday. Each day pull a daily, weekly, monthly, and semi-annual card. Work fast and don't worry about dirt; it will come up on your file.

Buy a card file container, two sets of colored index cards, and one set of dividers. Label one index divider "Daily." Then put the following items on white cards:

DAILY

1. Quickly pick up clutter in each room for five minutes.
2. Fix dinner after breakfast.
3. Pull monthly card.
4. Clean one drawer or one shelf in the kitchen.
5. Vacuum kitchen floor and do breakfast dishes.

WEEKLY (YELLOW CARDS)

Pull one of these cards each day. Try to have all the work on these cards completed by 11:00 a.m. each day. Then fix lunch and save the afternoons for fun projects.

MONDAY

1. Start wash. Do two batches each weekday.
2. Vacuum three rooms.
3. Dust three rooms.
4. Water plants and spray them.
5. Change two beds.
6. Pull monthly card.
7. Pull semi-annual card.
8. Empty waste baskets.
9. Sort laundry for tomorrow.

10. Unload dishwasher for morning.
11. Family home evening.

TUESDAY

Readjust these days to fit your own schedule of days for heavy work, days you may be gone for Relief Society, etc.

1. Start wash — two batches.
2. Clean bathroom thoroughly, scrubbing it completely.
3. Pull monthly card.
4. Sort laundry for tomorrow.
5. Work on church assignments.
6. Unload dishwasher for morning.
7. Wash living room and hall mirrors.

WEDNESDAY

1. Change two beds.
2. Dust three rooms.
3. Wash two batches of clothes.
4. Vacuum three rooms.
5. Pull monthly card and semi-annual card.
6. Prepare shopping list for the week.
7. Make menus for the week and tape them in the cupboards.
8. Take care of such things as checkbook, bills, birthdays, etc.
9. Clean refrigerator, wipe it out but don't defrost.
10. Water plants.
11. Sort laundry for tomorrow.
12. Unload dishwasher.

THURSDAY

1. Wash two batches of clothes.
2. Pull monthly card.
3. Do grocery shopping.

4. Sort laundry for tomorrow.
5. Unload dishwasher for morning.
6. Wash mirrors in upstairs bedroom.

FRIDAY
1. Change two beds.
2. Wash two batches of clothes.
3. Vacuum three rooms.
4. Dust three rooms.
5. Water plants.
6. Pull monthly and semi-annual cards.
7. Mending.
8. Scrub down the bathroom.
9. Sort laundry for tomorrow.
10. Unload dishwasher for morning.

SATURDAY
1. Prepare for Sunday (clothes and food).
2. Work on family home evening.
3. Have all dishes put away for Monday morning.

MONTHLY CARDS
Pull one of these cards each day (Monday through Friday).
After the first time through the job, each card should only take fifteen minutes. If it takes longer, file it under semi-annual. Rotate cards and file in back of section when finished. Because your work is being done on an even basis, this file eliminates spring cleaning and last-minute frustrations. Each line below goes on a separate blue card.

1. Vacuum mop boards in master bedroom closet.
2. Wash walls in master bedroom closet.
3. Scrub bathroom carpet.
4. Straighten one bedroom closet (make a card for each bedroom).

5. Straighten cleaning closet.
6. Clean bathroom sinks.
7. Clean shower curtains.
8. Wash master bedroom window — just wipe off glass. Make one card for every window in the house.
9. Straighten toy box.
10. Do three light fixtures. (Rotate until all light fixtures are washed.)
11. Scrub kitchen carpet.
12. Dust or wash knick knacks and their shelves.
13. Wash living room railing.
14. Clean phones.
15. Straighten husband's chest of drawers. (Make card for each family member.)
16. Straighten sewing closet and drawers.
17. Dust and clean inside of stereo.
18. Spot clean the carpet in one room. (Rotate until each room is done.)
19. Wash down washer, dryer, and freezer.
20. Straighten up washroom.
21. Straighten up fruit room.
22. Clean oven.
23. Clean top of fridge.
24. Dust plants.
25. Clean stove.
26. Dust off all pictures upstairs.
27. Dust off all pictures downstairs.
28. Scrub sliding doors thoroughly.
29. Do kitchen chairs thoroughly.
30. Do kitchen table thoroughly.
31. Do bar stools and bar thoroughly.
32. Clean fireplace.
33. Clean deck.

34. Wipe off vacuums.
35. Clean medicine cabinets.

SEMI-ANNUALLY

This card will take you longer than a monthly card. Such cards are days of heavy cleaning. These are on pink cards.

1. Defrost refrigerator.
2. Wash under and behind refrigerator.
3. Update cookbook and files.
4. Do one floor thoroughly — runs, mopboards, etc. (Make one card for each room.)
5. Upstairs bathroom window (whole treatment). (Make card for every room.)
6. Clean all the blankets in one room. (Make card for each room.)
7. Clean furnace room (filters, etc.)
8. Clean two doors thoroughly. (Rotate until all doors have been washed.)
9. Sort seasonal clothes.
10. Update photo and baby books.
11. Wash down furnace and hot water tank.
12. Clean garage.
13. Defrost freezer.
14. Every April, have sewing machine and typewriter serviced.
15. Do two walls in your house. (Rotate to complete all walls.)

Again, this file system is a suggestion. You must include areas specific to your needs or delete tasks that don't apply. Also, if you have children old enough for responsibility, you can have them take cards and/or delegate cards, etc.

If you are one of the matches and gasoline candidates, you probably need to read one of the books mentioned above. If you know how to clean and have been just plain lazy, you need to exercise more self-discipline.

Self-discipline is the ability to carry out a resolution once the mood is gone. You can get all charged up over the idea of cleaning your home, empty out all the closets, stock up on cleansers and polishes, start in, and then, as it becomes gut-level routine labor, just fizzle right out! DON'T DO THAT!

There is no greater feeling of accomplishment and self-worth than to have your home in order as a sparkling representative of who you are. Cleanliness of self, including the home, has always been considered as proceeding from a reverence to God. When the body and the environment are pure, the mind receives a comforter. Beauty most usually produces love, but cleanliness preserves it.

Benjamin Rumford, an English-American physicist wrote that "So great is the effect of cleanliness upon man, that it extends even to his moral character. Virtue never dwelt long with filth; nor do I believe there ever was a person scrupulously attentive to cleanliness who was a consumante villian."

Can you imagine President Kimball, or any of the General Authorities, living in a dirty, cluttered home? No, because it's out of character. You see, part of their character is REVERENCE.

For most of my life I had always regarded reverence as a state of being, an act. Then I read *A Reverent People* by President Spencer W. Kimball, and realized that reverence is a quality, a state of being, an attitude toward life.

> We are a richly blessed people. The Lord has given us everything: the gospel of Jesus Christ, the Light, the priesthood, the power, the promises, the covenants, the temples, our families, the truth. We should be the happiest people on earth. We should also be the most

reverent people, but here I think every individual and every family should take a look at themselves. Are we a reverent people? Do our actions in the home and at Church show reverence for our Creator?

. . . Many of our leaders have expressed regard for reverence as one of the *highest qualities* of the soul, indicating it involves true faith in God in his righteousness, high culture, and a love for the finer things in life . . . reverence toward the Father and the son is an essential *qualification* or *characteristic* of those who attain the celestial kingdom . . . We must remember that reverence is . . . not temporary behavior . . . True reverence involves . . . love, respect, gratitude . . . It is a virtue that should be part of our way of life. In fact, Latter-day Saints should be the most reverent people in all the earth." (pp. 1-2)

As I pondered the concept of reverence as a *quality*, I was reminded of the injunction which Moses received as he approached the burning bush: "Put off thy shoes from off thy feet, for the place whereon thou standst is holy ground" (Exodus 3:5).

As those beautiful words nourished my hungry soul, as they filled the open places of my mind, I considered the holy ground whereon I was often want to stand as I was witness to or participant in such sacred events as having one of my children nestled in my arms, receiving tender counsel from a loving parent, hearing that which is said before a sacred altar in a very sacred moment, seeing the support and compassion from a beloved friend, kneeling in humble prayer, or simply sitting quietly within my own home. These and other reverent moments have always been accompanied by strong feelings of self-worth and self-esteem. To be a reverent person is to possess those qualities. Don't you suppose that our Heavenly Father has reverence for all his creations, especially his home and being? Developing this QUALITY is to develop such love, respect, and gratitude for all of his creations. Those things over which you have immediate stewardship (your body and home) should be most sacred to you. You should regard your home and body as the Lord intends that you should. It should be the goal and commitment of every Latter-day Saint woman to be anxiously engaged in seeking to possess this quality.

"True reverence," continues President Kimball, "is a vital quality, but one that is fast disappearing in the world as the forces of evil broaden their influences. We cannot fully comprehend the power for good we can wield if the millions of members of Christ's true Church will serve as models of reverent behavior. We cannot imagine the additional numbers of lives we could touch. *Perhaps even more important, we cannot forsee the great spiritual impact on our own families* if we become the reverent people we know we should be." (p. 4)

Reverence comes from deep within, from a re-remembering, a sense of dignity and worth. It is a quality, to be developed and sought after. It is a vital force towards a strong self-image. It is a quality that God himself possesses. It is a quality which we MUST possess if we are to become like God.

Noble sisters, as you live your lives in pursuit of all that God desires for you, consider that the home wherein you stand is sacred ground.

Chapter  Six

Home, Sweeter Home

"Now we ask you to clean up. We urge each of you to dress and keep in a beautiful state the property that is in your hands."

—*Spencer W. Kimball*

Let me share with you a small story from the *Ensign Magazine* (July, 1980):

> For three days the paper daisy lay on the piano waiting for a more-deserved spot, some place where it could remind me of the message brought by my visiting teachers a few days earlier.
>
> I found the answer in my gloomy kitchen. It's dingy, white cabinets were scratched, out of date, and boring! The unmatched chairs around the table and the tarnished toaster only made the cupboards look worse. What a perfect place to plant a flower!
>
> Two pairs of flowered pillowcases, cut in half, hemmed, and decorated with ribbons, transformed the backs of my kitchen chairs. From the remaining cloth I made a toaster cover. Even the cabinets looked better in their

cheery surroundings.

And the Relief Society blossom taped to my refrigerator reminds me that help and *inspiration* come in a thousand different ways — even a single blossom can make a garden." (p. 68)

Inspiration! That is the word that makes life bubble and sing. Someone once said that "originality is nothing more than a pair of fresh eyes." I was once asked where my ideas come from. I answered that they came from other ideas!

Inspiration comes in a thousand different ways. The ideas in this chapter are meant to encourage and *inspire* you to new levels of creativity in personal expression in your home.

President Brigham Young said that we ought to "STUDY order and cleanliness . . . adorn your city and neighborhood. Make your home lovely, and adorn your hearts with the grace of God."

Study all that you can, prepare your minds, and then develop your personality in your home.

As the years have gone by, it has become increasingly more evident how much an attractive environment has to do with how a woman and the members of her family feel about themselves. There is no question that cheerful, pleasant surroundings promote the same cheerful, pleasant feelings within family members. The greatest rewards which I have experienced as a designer have not been monetary but in seeing the changes in people's lives as they move toward a better life style.

To a woman, "fulfilling the measure of her creation" involved pride in keeping her home clean and orderly, in entertaining others there, in developing her talents there, and in just plain loving her home. The husband and children will love to come home to an atmosphere conducive to love, enthusiasm, and productivity. I have seen it happen over and over again among many of the people with whom I have worked over the past ten or so years.

Making a home is simply the preparation of an environment. Why the word *prepare?* You prepare soil for planting, don't you? A cheerful and pleasant environment is the soil in which to plant the family. As they grow and develop, the blossoms appear — love, shared interests, the will to do better and to do more with life, and self-esteem.

Of course, there have been those who have acquired a larger home and fine furnishings simply for self-serving reasons. Many people with a poor self-image want a large house, fabulous furnishings, and several expensive cars and furs and jewelry by the trunkloads in order to say to the world: "Hey! Look at me, I'm important. I'm SOMEBODY. I'm successful." They suppose that money is synonymous with self-esteem.

It is not unrighteous to have thoughts of a better life or more material comfort. It is unrighteous, however, to have *only* those thoughts. Thoughts of success and luxury are normal and natural because they are God-given. Your Heavenly Father is not groveling in poverty to remain humble and spiritual. On the contrary, He lives in splendor and grandeur. The Lord said that He is preparing "mansions" for us to live in. *God is a success, and He wants us to be successful.* The good things of the earth are put here for man to enjoy, NOT FOR HIM TO INDULGE HIMSELF. If you are doing all that our Heavenly Father has asked — not part, but all — then it is appropriate to spend some concentration on temporal gain as well as spiritual.

"Therefore take no thought; saying, What shall we eat? or, What shall we drink? or, Wherewithal shall we be clothed? For your heavenly Father knoweth that ye have need of all these things. But seek ye first the kingdom of God and his righteousness, and all these things shall be added unto you" (3 Nephi 13:31-33).

I have found that to be a blessing true in my own life.

Many of my clients have been very affluent, and I have been privileged to do some interesting and exciting projects. However, no matter how wealthy a family is, there is always a limit or budget as to what they are willing to spend.

In budgeting expenses for decorating a home, whether it be just a "face lift" or a complete refurbishing, the first step is HONESTY with self. In dealing with people, no matter what their social standing is, they must be honest with themselves before I can help them.

I wish I had a dollar for every person that's walked through my home and said, "This isn't the way I thought an interior designer would live." They might be right! My home is understated, very simple (very little color), and planned exactly to the way we live. When we planned the house, we eliminated the formal dining room and the formal family room. We were honest about it. How often do we entertain? Perhaps once a month we invite close friends. In previous homes, the dining room always proved to be the biggest waste of space, and the furniture a fortune for as much use as it got. So, we built a big, country eat-in kitchen with used brick, glazed tile, copper ceilings, and a fresh country-floral print. It is where we eat every day, and it is elegant enough in a charming way that our guests feel comfortable and, indeed, entertained.

The living room was another waste of space. It has been our experience that the family never used the living room except on Monday evenings for family home evening. It, too, was a waste, and we were always tripping over toys in the family room. In the new home we eliminated the family room and have a large living-in room. It is very comfortable with high-beamed ceilings, wood floor, stucco walls, a big fireplace, and comfortable furniture. We use it everyday. The children respect it as a living room, and we enjoy it for all family activities.

Off of the childrens' bedrooms is a large room we call their playroom. The toys and projects remain there, and it has outside access.

As we discussed our life style, we planned our home accordingly. Both Steve and I work together in the design business (He's a graphic designer.), and we eat, breathe, and sleep color. When we come home we want a rest. Consequently, the house is in neutrals with shots of bright color here and there. The house was planned for our casual, relaxed, at-home living.

We also had to adapt to the reality of our life style even after we'd planned the house. We had decided to have a garden room off the master bedroom with a sitting area in it. The idea was to sit there and relax. After a while, we both realized we'd never just go out there and sit — too much to do — so we turned it into a room to hold more books!

Honesty is the key to a successful budget, not money. Most women don't run around the house in long, flowing gowns with a maribou collar and cuffs. Most are in jeans or pants and on the go. You must assess your life style and then style your home around that life.

A friend had an empty dining room for years. She was saving for a dining room set and hutch. One day she said to herself, I don't know why I'm saving for it. I never entertain that way. Maybe I think I will when I get the furniture, but I know I won't.

I asked her why she didn't just turn the room into something useful. They had been cramped for bedroom space for years and had let that room sit empty. Honesty with herself produced a study from that empty space that left the bedrooms free of the desks.

No matter whether your home is a cottage or a palace, you must make the effort to make it an environment conducive to love, cheerfulness, and productivity.

In our early years of marriage, we were students at Brigham Young University. We had a small baby and lived in a basement apartment. You know the kind — a drain in the middle of the kitchen floor, no carpets, weeds growing through the wall in the shower, and if you turned off all the lights in the middle of the day, it was as dark as in the middle of night.

My mother came to help me with that new baby, and she stayed long enough to use her skills and talents in helping me make that cave exhibit some cheerfulness and personality. Together we painted walls, made curtains (It didn't take much; the windows were only a foot square.), and a slipcover for the plastic sofa that was cracked and split. A few toss pillows, bright, cheery paint, a colorful tablecloth, a basket of dried flowers, and the apartment began to look like a home. We didn't have any money (We were just poor university students.), so Mother contributed the total cost of $80, for which I will always be grateful. That was thirteen years ago, and inflation would make that figure somewhat higher today. The point is that with a little creativity and proper planning, even a shack can look charming and cozy on just a few dollars and lots of inspiration!

We do a lot of model homes for builders. They are always on a budget! They want the greatest look for fifty cents and so we try. Over the past few years we have become expert in decorating on tight budgets. I want to share some of my ideas with you so that no matter how tight your budget is, you can do something about your home and have a better place in which to live. But first, in order to give you more insight and better aid your creativity, you need some understanding of *design* and some guidelines to follow.

Like dressing "classic," there is a standard in the home furnishings industry that is called "eclectic." It means a collected look, not thrown together, but rather it looks as if each piece were carefully chosen for that particular place in the room. It is a timeless look. It does not boast of style but rather mood and feeling. In fifty years, such rooms will still be in style. The fabrics and colors may come and go, but the feeling is always right. An eclectic room is a mixture of traditional and contemporary mood, or an Oriental, French, or Spanish mood. The style of the furnishings will wary and each bespeak importance and personality. The pictures below are "styled" rooms.

These pictures are "eclectic" rooms.

So, how do you determine what is a good choice and what is not a good choice? It's a matter of taste. Good taste is not something we are born with, it is something we develop. Conversely, we can develop bad taste. So how do we develop good taste, which is the ability to discern and appreciate quality, beauty, order, and whatever constitutes excellence? Good taste is not acquired by accepting every new trend and fad that comes along. It is gained by a constant and deliberate process of first becoming acclimated to or aware of design and then training the eye to distinguish between what is and what is not good design.

Here are some basic guidelines to help you:

1. First study and understand the principles and elements of interior design as discussed later in this chapter.
2. Apply the principles to all your analyses of design. Practice observing and critiquing until design, which has been *recognized* over the years as good design, becomes good to you.
3. Make it a deliberate effort to observe surroundings carefully. Visit model homes often and look for light, shadow, shape, texture, pattern, color, size, and scale. Notice what colors do to each other. Notice balance, proportion, focal points.
4. Subscribe to magazines about decorating and then digest them, realizing that not everything in magazines represents good taste. Study historical and contemporary styles and interiors. Visit furniture stores and model homes. Find an interior designer you like and trust. Interview her. Ask questions and observe, observe, observe. Most designers are willing to help educate the public.
5. Pay particular attention to accessories. As you look through magazines and see rooms that appeal to you,

notice the accessories. Take note of how they accent a table or draw a color into view. Be aware of what kind of things are used for accessories and the kind of personality (if any) that they give the room. For example, can you guess what the people who live there are like simply by looking at the accessories?

6. Fads, or current trends, are not good indicators of good taste. Some fashions will soon be outdated.

7. Good taste is not determined by cost or even quality. I have seen some hideous designs that were very well constructed and had a very high price tag.

8. Be honest with yourself about your way of life. If you don't go around the house in a long, flowing hostess gown, don't plan your house or make choices for that kind of life style. When you choose and live with things appropriate to your way of life, you express your own taste and talents.

PRINCIPLES AND ELEMENTS OF DESIGN

In order to understand good versus poor design, you must acquaint yourself with the basic principles and elements that are in a design composition.

Proportion and Scale mean the relationship of one object to the whole room or to another object, i.e., a sofa in relationship to a living room, etc. It was the Greeks who discovered the secret of good proportion, and they called it the Golden Mean. They found, for example, that the square is the least pleasant proportion for a room — rectangle being better — and that the division of a line somewhere between one-half and one-third its length is most pleasing.

Tieback holder is placed between ½ and ⅓ distance from floor to ceiling.

Remember this when hanging pictures, deciding molding, placing mirrors, etc.

Scale is the overall size of an object compared to other objects. For example, two sofas may have the same dimensions but look different because one is dainty with French legs, and the other is heavily tufted and upholstered. Keeping scale in mind as you design your home, you will want to avoid huge furniture in small rooms; avoid small, delicate furniture in large rooms; keep furniture on the same scale by avoiding having a dainty end table next to a huge sofa or a spindly lamp on a massive table; and finally, you will want to keep patterns in scale relative to the piece of furniture or wall next to which it is to be used.

Large pattern on a vaulted wall balances with a large-scale hutch.

Every room needs a sense of *balance*. It is the sense of weight, as the eye perceives it. There are two types of balance: formal, which requires that identical objects be arranged in the same manner on either side of an axis; or informal, which, though it requires more thought and imagination, is more interesting. Informal balance is achieved when objects of different sizes, shapes, and colors balance each other. Two small objects may balance a larger one — a shiny, small one may balance a larger, dull one, or a large object moved closer to a central point will balance a smaller one pushed farther away from that point.

Note of warning: The use of too many pairs in a room may produce boredom.

Opposite walls should balance each other. Don't line large furniture on one side.

Furniture should present a pleasant distribution of high and low, large and small objects.

Most rooms need a mixture of both formal and informal balance.

Rhythm is the ease with which the eye moves either within a room or from one room to another. The repetition of color, pattern, texture, etc., generally adds to rhythm. For example, if the carpet is the same color throughout the house, the house appears larger, and the eye is able to move easily about. Rhythm also creates a mood from room to room.

The *focal point* is the center of interest in a room. It is the point to which the eye is continually drawn (a fireplace, large window, an outside view, the furniture grouping itself, a collection, a bookshelf, an armoire, an art object, a colorful rug, etc.).

The focal point in this room is the rug.

Harmony is the unity or the unifying theme created in a room or home. Molded plastic chairs, for example, do not belong against a wall of formal French paneling. Furniture should reflect the architecture of the room. Colors should reflect the mood of the room, and the more traditional the room, the more subdued the colors. Fabrics should also be in harmony with the furniture style. Herculon, for example, is not the fabric to have on a French chair. Windows should also be decorated with fabrics suitable to style — a dressy fabric doesn't belong in a rustic cottage.

Having briefly reviewed the principles of design, we now turn to *design elements.*

Texture is the surface quality of fabrics, walls, objects, etc. It has nothing to do with elegance, for a heavy, hand-hewn texture can be even more elegant than smooth velvet. The textures in a room should be mixed inasmuch as all shiny or all rough fabric is boring. However, be sure to mix compatable textures. Don't use satin and herculon together or velvet and burlap.

Line has to do with the direction the eye travels around and up and down furniture, objects, walls, and so on. Lines in a room are either curved, vertical, horizontal, diagonal, or radial. One important thing to remember about line is to make sure that the furniture isn't all low or all high. Too many diagonal lines in a room result in an unsettled appearance. Vertical lines add height. It is preferable to mix vertical, diagonal, horizontal, and curved lines in a room.

Space and *Shape* have to do with the areas created by furniture arrangement, architecture, etc. Empty areas also have shape. Shape is the actual angle and size of the objects in the room. It is important to avoid too many different sizes and shapes in a room as this can be confusing to the eye. Negative space is pleasing so don't feel like you have to fill up every nook and cranny with pictures, tables, plants, and Aunt Matilda's old chair!

Light, the brightness or darkness of a room, created by artificial or natural light, intensity of color, amount of color, etc., is also important. Be sure to provide adequate lighting for reading and work areas. Conversation areas require less light. In bathrooms, overhead lighting casts shadows on the face and makes shaving or putting on make-up difficult. Bedrooms should also have adequate light (particularly at night) for seeing into clossets or dressers. Bedside lighting should be provided for "effect" and for reading. To make a small room appear larger, paint the walls and ceiling dark, keep the floor dark, and keep the lighting more toward the center of the room. The walls will "disappear."

Fabrics, patterns, and *prints* are used on walls, furniture, floors, windows, etc. Patterns used in the same room must have a pleasing relationship to each other. A common element (color, texture, motif) should tie them together. The principal pattern need not be repeated in the room if one or more of the colors in the pattern are carried over into the room. Repeating the pattern on more than one piece or on all the pieces or on the windows and walls gives a unified effect and may be used to unify odd pieces of furniture. Nevertheless, avoid garrish, loud, or trite prints and do not have more than one bold print in a room. Use other patterns to complement the dominant one. When combining fabrics, use ones that are suitable for each other. (An informal, bold floral needs plaids, stripes, and heavy textures as a complement, while a pastel cotton damask would require more delicate companion fabrics.)

Light fabrics lighten a room, whereas dark ones darken it. You can also make a room casual or dressy by your choice of fabrics. Pay attention to the "mood" of the room and don't put a contemporary print with a traditional one. When using wallpaper, try to use matching fabrics to create large-looking rooms. Ugly windows can be hidden with good print and drapery treatment, or you can show off a beautiful window or view with a delicate and plain fabric. The repeated use of the same fabric can also tie several "hodgepodge" rooms together. Relieve a dull, blah room by adding a collection of brightly colored print pillows in complementary colors. For example, if you have beige carpet, a gold sofa, and beige walls, get a print that has beige, a little gold, lots of brown, copper, and some blue and then make pillows to splash on the sofas and chairs! You can even alter the size of a clumsy, bulky piece of furniture by choosing a plain, medium-colored fabric or one with a small overall print. Use fabrics you can live with and enjoy. If the velvet sofa will never be used because of the kids, don't buy it! Avoid the hideous herculon prints in heavy gold, green, or turquoise!

Color should reflect your personality in the main living areas as well as in the private areas. Don't choose a color because Mildred, your neighbor, has it. Choose your favorite colors! Choose a *color scheme* from a fabric, wallpaper, picture, rug, magazine picture, or from your favorite colors. Pull out a dominant color and then two or three supportive colors. It is important that you keep from having competing colors in the same room. Do not, for example, have equal amounts of two colors. If you are inexperienced with color, use the most neutral color in the color scheme for the floors and walls. Warm, off-whites are also easier to work with and blend with other colors than cool off-whites. Warm, off-whites generally have beige, yellow, or pink casts, and cool off-whites have blue, gray, or green casts. Brighter, darker colors used in large areas are less demanding than the same colors used in small areas. Color also appears stronger when covering a large area such as walls or a carpet. It is possible to lower a ceiling that is too high simply by painting it a darker color than the walls. Conversely, you can raise a ceiling that is too low simply by painting it lighter than the walls. The color of the draperies should either blend with the carpet or the walls. If a print is used, it should be repeated on a piece of furniture. Otherwise, all you see is a printed drapery in a room. Don't make every room in the house a different color. Repeat colors from room to room for the sake of harmony

Living Room
- Beige carpet
- Beige walls
- Off-white sofa
- Beige and blue floral chair with a little plum
- Plum accessories

Kitchen
- Off-white linoleum
- Cranberry, beige, and light blue wallpaper
- Cranberry and blue accessories

Bath
- Beige carpet
- Navy blue, beige, and rust wallpaper
- Rust towels

Bedroom
- Beige carpet
- Blue, grasscloth wallcovering
- Beige, powder blue, and lemon yellow draperies and bedspread
- Lemon yellow accessories

Were you to walk from room to room, you would sense that beige and blue are the unifying colors. Each room has its own personality and accent colors, but the whole house seems to flow together.

GUIDELINES FOR GOOD FLOOR PLANS

In arranging the floor plan for your home, the key words are efficiency, beauty, and good design. Nevertheless, it is the life style of the family which must be given top priority. These are some hints on planning a floor plan:

1. Have a plan. You may not be able to afford to do a room all at once but plan it as though you will. You can then safely proceed with purchases. Too often women buy a sofa, then try to find something to go with it and can't, or choose a wallpaper and later try to decide on draperies.

2. Study the room carefully. Look at the light exposure, traffic areas, height, width, length, etc.
3. Draw the room to scale. Draw the outline of the room freehand on a piece of paper. Include all the openings, windows, jogs, etc. With a tape measure, go around and measure each line and opening on your paper and write down the measurement by that line. Take one-fourth inch graph paper (each square is one-fourth inch square) and, using the graph paper and a ruler, draw your room according to your measurements with one-fourth inch (or one square) being equal to one foot.

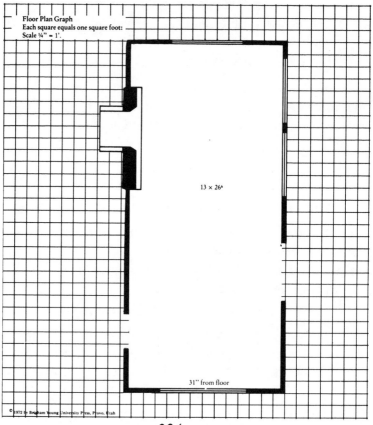

Floor Plan Graph
Each square equals one square foot:
Scale ¼" = 1'.

13 × 26⁶

31" from floor

4. Group the furniture. Cut out the templates on the following pages and arrange the furniture according to your guidelines. Place large pieces first, chairs second, tables and lighting third, etc. For specific areas, here are some additional pointers:

ENTRY:
•Keep uncluttered
•Depending on size, a chair or small entry table is nice
•Possibly a bench or console
•Lighting should be dramatic

LIVING ROOM:
•Decide how room will be used
•Create conversation areas
•Keep a focal point in mind (window, fireplace, bookshelf) and have the furniture arranged so as to enhance the focal point
•Traffic areas should not go through conversation areas and those areas should be cozy and intimate with seating placed close together
•Tables should "anchor" larger pieces and provide good lighting
•Avoid hanging mirrors where people can see themselves when they eat or talk
•Soft lighting but not gloomy
•If possible, group furniture around the fireplace

FAMILY ROOM:
•If television is the center of attention, the furniture must allow for ease of viewing
•Adequate book and/or game storage
•If piano is there, place so as to be out of traffic and conversation areas
•Lighting should be brighter than living room

BEDROOM:
- Beds placed first
- Determine traffic lanes
- Then auxiliary pieces

MISCELLANEOUS:
- Shapes such as rectangles and ovals are more pleasing than squares and circles (pictures, tables, etc.)
- Rough textures require heavier objects than smooth textures
- Pictures should be hung no more than six to nine inches above sofa or table
- Pictures hung on an empty wall should be at eye level (about five feet)

BEDROOM

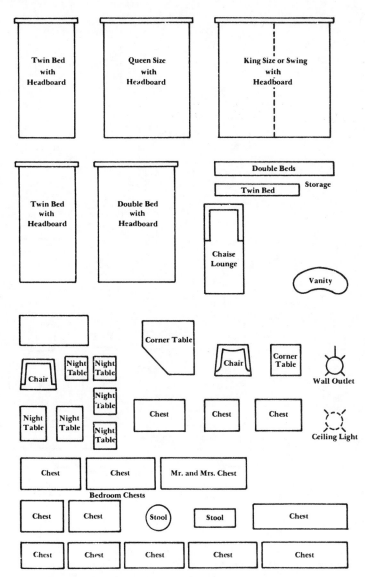

DINING ROOM

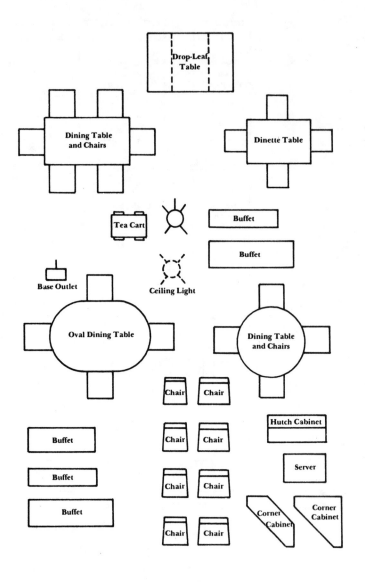

Courtesy of Better Homes and Gardens
© 1972 by Brigham Young University Press, Provo, Utah

LIVING ROOM

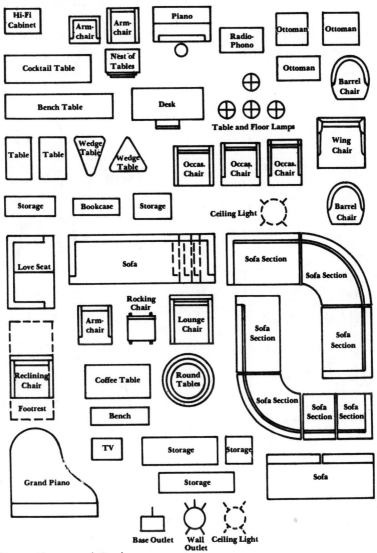

Courtesy of Better Homes and Gardens
©1972 by Brigham Young University Press, Provo, Utah

STORAGE

Usually a woman's first problem with a house is storage.

Closets are usually poorly designed. However, they can be made more functional. The closet in the following photo has been redesigned for more efficiency and might, for example, be most suited for a teenage girl.

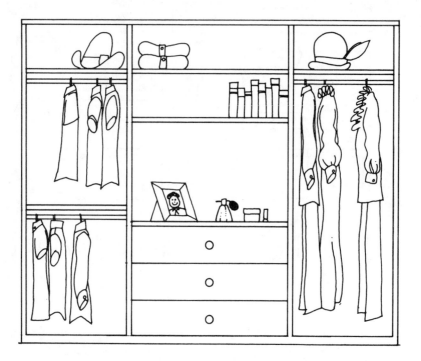

The closet was divided into thirds. The original pole was used and also divided into thirds. Two of the divisions were used for skirts, pants, blouses (hung double), and the other division was used for long dresses. The dresser was put in the closet and extra shelves built. The original amount of hanging space was maintained, but plenty of shelves for storage were added. Moving the dresser out of the room gave her more space in the bedroom for a desk.

Master bedroom closets are another place to double-hang men's shirts and pants as well as ladies' skirts and blouses.

Children rarely have much to hang up, and yet I always see that long pole in a ten foot or twelve foot closet. The drawing in the photo below represents one possibility for adapting a child's closet.

One lady in a small, three-room home had three little girls, no family room or playroom, and only a tiny living room. By changing closets, she put all three children in one bedroom and used the second bedroom as a playroom. We completely removed closet shelves, doors, and the pole in one bedroom closet and made it into an alcove for the crib. In the other bedroom, we moved the girls' clothes into the closet along with toys and books and turned that bedroom into a playroom.

Sometimes in an extra bedroom that's not in use (when a

child has left home), we've again gutted the closet and turned it into a television, stereo, or library area. Sometimes a hall closet has been turned into a sewing center. Assess your needs and then plan the changes and make your closets more useful.

Tables can also be used for storage.

Take an old chest (with drawers), remove the legs, and you have night stands or end tables with drawers.

An old wicker basket used for storage in the laundry or for costumes makes an excellent place to store blankets, food, etc. They can also be used as end tables or night stands. I have two that I paid four dollars for at Deseret Industries.

Old army trunks, purchased at a surplus store, can be sprayed shiny, bright enamel colors and used with or without glass tops as cocktail tables, night stands, or end tables. They are great for storing bedding, linens, clothes, or food.

Hinged, homemade plywood boxes can be used to store many things. Make them eighteen inches high, 36 inches deep, and 65 inches to 72 inches long. Paint or wallpaper the sides and use a foam cushion seat two to four inches thick and back pillows, slipcovered in a colorful sheet, and you have an instant sofa storage unit.

Hinged plywood boxes, 24 inches wide, sixteen inches high, and 48 inches deep, covered with paper or paint, topped with a two inch cushion, and outfitted with four heavy-duty casters, make excellent "rolling" storage units that can also be used as seating for the kitchen table or the patio table.

Metal food storage containers, sprayed with bright colors, make great night stands for kids' rooms. They can be stacked two deep if necessary. Four to six of them also look great, enameled and with a piece of glass across the top, as a cocktail table.

You can place a trunk at the foot of a bed for extra storage and even put a cushion on top to make a place to sit down and tie or untie shoes.

A round table with legs and covered with a cloth that goes to the floor can even be used for hiding various items.

Use an empty corner to build in a V-shaped desk or a worktable with a chair or shelves tucked underneath.

Walls offer other storage possibilities. For example, an empty wall that is positioned in such a way as not to allow furniture against it can be used for bookshelves. If there is a door in the middle of the wall, build around it.

It is also a good idea to rearrange existing shelves so that they're only slightly taller than the objects they hold. You will probably be able to add more shelves. Also, use the floor as the bottom shelf.

Hidden storage space can also be achieved by hanging louvered shutters or doors from shelf to shelf or from floor to ceiling. Or, easier still, a matchstick bamboo shade hung from a high shelf can be rolled down to conceal your things.

You can build shelves around a sofa or over a toilet. The latter shelves can be used for baskets of cosmetics, washcloths, soaps, etc.

New *grid racks* are nothing more than industrial grids and can be purchased inexpensively at any industrial furniture company or department store. They have hundreds of uses. You can put one over a stove for utensils, hot pads, pans, etc. Larger grids can be hung on ceilings to hold strings of onions, garlic, herbs, or pans on hooks. Small grids between cabinets and counter tops can be used to hold spices, utensils, etc. In a child's room or in the bathroom, they can be used to hold supplies, toys, etc. They can even be put in an entryway for hats and coats.

Baskets offer a very tasteful selection of storage possibilities. Square straw or plastic baskets can be hung on the walls for extra storage, or they can be used for living room plants or for books, records, etc. Toys, sweaters, and books can also be stored in them in childrens' rooms. They can also provide kitchen storage space for cookbooks, salad bowls, dishes, and other items. Wall-hung bicycle baskets make great storage in bathrooms for rolled-up, colorful towels, for grooming gear, or for colored soaps.

Other storage ideas include building a platform bed or seat with both sides hinged for easy access.

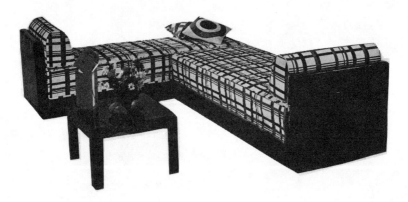

Suitcases can be stored inside a headboard (ten or more inches in width). Use the top of the headboard as a place for books and a lamp.

Skirt a leggy bathroom sink with shirred fabric held on by glue or heavy elastic banding. Store soaps, paper products, and other supplies underneath.

Use the dead space above wall-hung bathroom or kitchen cabinets for dry goods or food storage which has been emptied into attractive jars or containers. You might also use the area for sewing trays, vases, or seldom-used dishes that take up a lot of cabinet space.

FLOORS

With the price of floor coverings these days, a person is often left to "make do."

If you have worn traffic patterns by entrances, pick a complementary color to your present carpet and purchase a strip of carpet at a local carpet remnant store. Carpet comes in rolls that are twelve feet wide, so a strip that is two or three feet wide would do an average room. The heights of the piles should be fairly compatible, but it is not an absolute necessity. Cut back one foot of the carpet all around the edge of the room and seam a one-foot border around the perimeter (see photo below). If the carpet is not worn — just a tired color — cut the border one foot in, leaving the outside border in the main color. Then inset the border of new color.

The border also gives an area rug look and can introduce another color into a drab room.

Rugs made of carpet patches are often dizzy and obnoxious, but a large-scale version done on a diagonal can be exciting. Buy three remnants (never more than three colors) and cut them at diagonals, seam them together, and install them as you would one piece of carpet. Colors should be complementary like brown, tan, and beige or pale gray, dark gray, and cream, etc.

For worn linoleum or the carpet in a family room, make a room-size area rug with remnants and then border it as suggested above.

For the stairs to a basement, use scraps and make your own rainbow by covering each step in a different color.

To recarpet children's rooms inexpensively, look for ads in bargain newspapers for carpet from someone's living room. Living rooms are bigger than small bedrooms, and you can usually cut around worn spots. Such carpets also don't get a lot of wear as a general rule, and the main parts of the carpet are in good condition.

Inexpensive straw (sisal) matting purchased at an import shop or carpet company is a great floor covering for play rooms, family rooms, trailers, and children's rooms.

Stained concrete, for a contemporary look in homes with concrete floors, is another option for floors that need help. A product called Kemiko is an acid stain available in thirty colors that eats the concrete and leaves a marbelized effect. A heavy Kemiko paste is then applied and buffed (about ten coats), and the effect is a no-care floor that may (with heavy traffic) need to be waxed every two or three years. We did this to the concrete in our showroom, and it looks like marble and is beautiful. The address for the stain and the wax is: Kemiko, 2213 North Tyler Avenue, South El Monte, California 91733.

You must follow the instructions meticulously. The acid

spends itself quickly. The cost to do an average twelve by fourteen room is about $25.

Old wood plank floors can be sanded and painted with an acrylic paint — solid color — and sealed with polyurethane sealer. This gives you an easy-care floor with a tough finish. You can also strip those drab plank floors, leave them natural, and finish with satin sealer, which gives a great natural look.

Remnant stores have sales which means, since remnants are already reduced, that you can find some real bargains!

Finally, keep floor coverings simple and avoid the multi-colored or multi-patterned specials! A simple floorcovering is a nicer background for all the other elements in the home. Usually, the over-patterned numbers are poorly designed, both in patterns and colors!

WINDOWS

To measure for draperies, measure (in inches) the desired width of the drapery, measure (in inches) the desired length of the drapery, add twelve inches to the width (six inches for each side return and six inches for the overlap in the center), then divide eighteen into the total drapery width (18" is the allowance for two and one-half times fullness for a width of fabric). If the fabric is less than 48 inches wide, reduce the figure from 18 inches to 16 inches. The answer, after dividing by 18 is the number of widths or panels of fabric needed to go across the window. To find the yardage, take the measured length and add 18 inches (18 inches is ten inches for a double-turned hem and eight inches for a double-turned heading). The total of the measured length and the 18 inches is what the *cut length* is or the length you cut each width or panel of fabric. Now, multiply the number of widths or panels by the cut length, and the answer will be the total of running inches you need. Divide your answer by 36 (36 inches per yard), and the result is the number of yards you need.

If there is a pattern repeat, you must *add* that repeat length to the cut length.

A lot of fabric can be gained in sheets. Below is a chart which tells the yardage for various sizes of sheets.

	Cut Size before hemming	Approximate yardage per sheet and pillowcase
Twin Flat Sheet	66 × 104	4-1/5
Double Flat Sheet	81 × 104	5-1/5
Queen Flat Sheet	90 × 110	6
King Flat Sheet	108 × 110	7-1/8
Regular Pillowcase	42 × 36	7/8
King Size Pillowcase	42 × 46	1-1/5

If you can't sew French pleated draperies, there are some great window treatments that even a beginner can handle.

A *rod pocket top* requires a one- or two-inch wooden dowel that is to be used as the rod, with two brackets on each side to hold it up. Fold the fabric over on top and sew a "pocket" wide enough to go over the rod. Make the side hems and then push the rod through the pocket, gathering the fabric tightly, and then hang it up. See page 244 for a sample picture.

You can also make a pocket on the bottom and make a curtain from the floor to the ceiling or one for just the inside of the window itself (see page 244).

If you use a sheet, the large, pre-hemmed edge of the sheet can act as the bottom hem of the drapery — EASY!

The *tuxedo drape* is a very tailored, yet simple window treatment which is great for apartments or mobile homes where space is at a minimum. This type of drape looks conservative

The photo above demonstrates a rod pocket top. The picture at left shows a curtain from floor to ceiling.

without all that fabric hanging at the windows. These are also measured in FLAT widths, not using any fullness.

Sew two flat pieces of fabric together, either the same fabric or two complementary types, and leave a small pocket at the top for the flat dime store variety curtain rod. Make the drapery to just cover the window. This style works best on long, narrow windows. Sew a small, gold hook or ring to the inside edge one-third of the way up from the hem. Then fold back to reveal the inside fabric and hook it on the other side of the drapery.

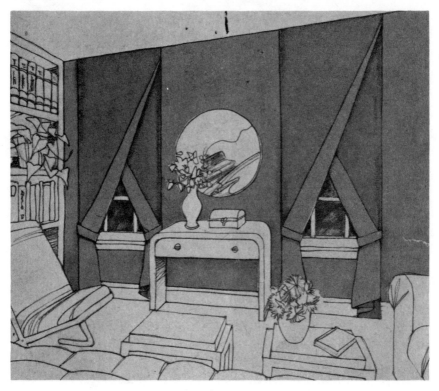

Tuxedo Drapes

Tuxedo Drapes

Stationary side tiebacks are particularly suited to windows that do not pose a sun or privacy problem. Such "fake" draperies can soften a window without the expense of full drapes.

Make two rod pockets top (#1) draperies with one king sheet cut in half. Hang on opposite sides of the window and tie back.

A bamboo matchstick blind gives a great look for under ten dollars. They can be purchased at any discount store, and if the exact size you need isn't in stock, buy larger ones and simply cut them down with ordinary garden scissors but cut equal amounts off of each side. Hang baskets and plants in the room with wicker accents, and you have a charming window treatment. They can also be spray painted in great colors! To dress them up, use either stationary side tiebacks (see above) or hourglass, unbleached muslin in a rod pocket *top* and *bottom* effect.

Mini-blinds are inexpensive, metal one-inch blinds that keep heat and cold out and provide full viewing ability through the window when the blades are open. They come in about 100 decorator colors, and for a complete window treatment, they are very inexpensive. There are two guidelines: (1) they look best when installed INSIDE the window casing or frame and (2) they should blend with the wall color or the *main* color in the wallpaper. NEVER use them as the "accent" color.

Fabric-covered shutters are also easy to make. Measure the window and then divide it into equal parts of two, four, six, or eight. Have plywood cut to fit the divisions and then completely cover each piece of wood with fabric (or wallpaper) and hinge them together with piano hinges. Hang the panels with covered hanging strips and hinges on each side of the window.

Fake Roman shades are made like tuxedo drapery except that every twelve inches or so, a pocket is made for the narrow wooden dowel (about one-fourth inch in diameter). Start and end with dowel and divide the rest of the length so that you come out with even spacing between dowels, no closer together than twelve inches and no farther apart than twenty inches. Attach nails or hooks on each side of the window and catch the dowels on the nails.

Plants can also double as window coverings. Hang plants at different levels in front of a window for a "curtain of plants." Glass shelves in front of a window with plants on them, also make great window coverings.

A garden trellis, which can be purchased at a hardware or garden store in four by eight sheets for under ten dollars, can also serve as a fine window covering. Painted or stained and put in a frame, it can be cut to size. The frame can be hinged on one side to allow for movability in cleaning or opening windows. For a shutter effect, use two for a double-hung shutter. Another "trellis" effect can be achieved with baby gates, the kind that are hinged to doorways and fold like an accordian. Cup racks hooked together also make a great treatment for a small bathroom window, and you can even hang plants from them. See example photograph on the following page.

WALLS AND CEILINGS

For years I've told my clients that if the walls, floors, and ceilings are attractive, the room is pretty even if there isn't any furniture in it. Too many people ruin their rooms by overdoing the walls and floors and almost completely ignoring the ceiling.

In choosing wallpaper, stay away from corny or novelty prints like the salt and pepper shakers or the roosters for the kitchen, the powderpuff ladies for the bath, or the "cutesy" prints for the children's rooms.

Remember scale and proportion. It may look like a huge pattern in the wallpaper book because you are looking at it in relation to a 20 inch by 24 inch page. Picture it on a twelve foot by twelve foot wall.

It is also best to avoid flashy and neon-colored splashes that you may quickly grow tired of, and for walls with a ceiling over ten feet in height (sloped ceiling), avoid paper with a lot of pattern. A grasscloth or plain print is a better choice.

Don't mix papers in one room unless you are using a chair-rail molding. Yes, the wallpaper book shows all those papers together, but look again. They are usually in architecturally interesting rooms that have natural breaks. In rooms with four straight walls like most homes, putting one paper on one wall and another pattern on an opposite wall only shrinks the room and makes it look cluttered.

A great way to enhance wallpaper is to use it with a chairrail molding. Put the molding 36 inches from the floor all the way around the room and use a small, complementary mini-print below the molding (or a complementary color of paint) and a stronger pattern above.

Remember to keep a dominant color scheme. This involves, among other things, keeping the main color in the paper in harmony with the carpet color. In bathrooms, kitchens, or in any room with a small, spare or chopped-up wall space or area, use an overall pattern on *all* the walls as well as the ceiling. Suddenly, corners and jogs disappear, and the room appears larger.

Buy paper, if possible, from a reputable store with a reputable design staff. Design services are usually free, and the price of the paper in the wallpaper book is the same as in the paint store. If the paint store will discount it ten percent and the designer won't, go with the designer because ten percent is a small price to pay for his or her expert advice.

Shop for design and color, not price. If you can't afford a well-designed paper for all the walls, paper just one wall and paint the others or save your money until you can. Stay out of those stack 'em deep and sell 'em cheap stores. The papers there are usually very poorly designed. Even closeouts from big companies can be a problem because those papers were so awful they never sold. If you can't afford decent paper, don't paper — just paint. A beautiful color on a wall is much better than a tacky wallpaper print!

Fabric, especially sheets, can go a long way on less money and give a warmer look than paper. Here are some methods of applying fabric to walls:

1. Shirring — make a pocket on the top and the bottom of the fabric, gather on rods, then attach the rods at the baseboards and the ceiling;
2. Velcro — sew velcro on the wrong side of the fabric along the edges, glue more velcro on the walls, and then attach the velcro pieces to each other;
3. Staple gun — staple the top first, then the bottom, and the sides last. (Exposed staples can be hidden with molding or braid.); and
4. Paste — put a coat of paste on the wall and let it set until tacky, place fabric strip on wall (start at the top and ease fabric down), and with a brush work the wrinkles out toward the side seams. Trim rough edges with straight edge and razor blade.

Paint is coming back. A beautiful color in the right finish and with the right lighting can produce a gorgeous effect.

When you're selecting paint, choose paint that is three shades lighter than the chip. It darkens in large areas. Also select a flat finish (latex flat) for darker colors although it is harder to care for. A shiny finish in a dark color can look garrish. If you will be using several gallons for one job, mix them all together in a larger container to assure even color. Finally, you might consider painting the ceiling and walls the same color to create the effect of more spaciousness. For real space enlargement, match to carpet color.

Try some fresh color schemes:

1. Tan walls, navy carpet, navy draperies, tan upholstery, creamy white moldings and accessories, red or rust throw pillows

2. Camel walls and carpet, eggshell ceiling, creamy white semi-gloss molding, pink or salmon cotton duck upholstery, navy blue accessories

3. Off-white tile or linoleum, walls, ceiling, and draperies; off-white bedspread or upholstery; raspberry accessories and pillows; lots of green plants

4. Silver gray carpet and ceiling; ivory stucco walls; salmon, mauve, gray, and plum fabric; deep plum accessories

5. Mauve walls, floors, and mini-blinds; oyster ceilings; deep hunter green bedspread; chair in hunter green and white check; pure white accessories

6. Try black as an accent color for a dramatic room — camel walls and floor; ivory ceiling, camel cotton duck upholstery; camel draperies trimmed with black band on hem; wicker furniture lacquered black; dull and shiny black accessories; one bowl of red flowers on cocktail table. (Soft peach could be substituted for the camel or beiges, grays, pale greens or blues, mauves — any soft color.)

7. To make elegant master bath — off-white carpet, sinks, cabinets, and tub; peach grasscloth on walls and ceilings; wine-colored towels and accessories; or pastel blue ceiling; apricot walls and floors; robin's egg blue background floral fabric; lemon yellow accessories

8. Try a primary color scheme (called Hi-Tech Look) — stripped oak plank floor (strip down your old varnished plank floors, leave natural, and seal with a flat floor sealer; large pillows (back pillows in solid colors of red, yellow, and blue); baskets on walls in red, yellow, and blue; a big basket of silk flowers (in red, yellow, and blue) on cocktail table

9. Shell carpet; shell furniture; deep apricot and teal blue

accents
10. Beige walls and ceilings; brown carpet; natural canvas upholstery; shades of raspberry, mauve, aubergine, and turquoise accents
11. Pale yellow walls; pale apricot ceiling; celery green carpet; darker shades of green, apricot, and yellow furniture; white moldings and accessories; lots of plants; bright lemon yellow flowers and pillows
12. To enlarge a small room, like an apartment or mobile home, or to camouflage bad walls — chocolate brown carpet; chocolate brown walls; oyster ceiling; rough-sawn wood whitewashed for molding and book shelves; chocolate brown upholstery (furniture fades into carpet and walls look smaller); bright raspberry pillows and flowers); accessorize with brass, mirror tables, and white
13. Paint a graphic on a wall with masking tape and small rollers using your favorite colors

You can also create new effects with molding and print combined. For example, put chairrail molding around dining room or child's room to create interest, then paper or paint above and below it. You can also create a headboard with molding (see photo at right).

Create a wall treatment with vertical or diagonal molding by painting the wall and molding all one color for an interesting textural effect. Molding and a mirror together also create an architectural effect.

Common redwood or fir benderboard, used for forming sidewalks and pools, etc., is great paneling either natural or painted. It can be used horizontally, vertically, randomly, diagonally, or in a herringbone pattern.

Left natural, it gives a more casual, rougher, country look. Painted, it is more dressy. It can be painted with a solid color paint, or it can be painted with a watery mixture (three parts paint and one part water — *off-white paint only* for this); and after it dries, the grain stands out, and the boards have a weathered or whitewashed look. It's a beautiful effect. I used this off-white weathered look in one of my bedrooms. The walls were done on a diagonal with peach carpet, peach satin moire, ecru eyelet, and lace. The mixture of the soft, washed, rough wood with dressy feminine fabrics was gorgeous!

Ceiling can also be bordered with molding for a more finished look. To lower a flat ceiling that is too high, bring molding down twelve inches (on the walls) and paint the border and the ceiling the same color. Paint the wall that is below the molding a darker color.

Avoid the four by eight sheets of cheap wood paneling — especially the dark, dreary variety. They generally have no style, no charm, no character, no quality, no design. If you need to cover bad walls, either save your money and sheetrock, use shirred sheets top and bottom, staple up fabric panels, or stucco them. Use anything but that awful dark plastic!

For stucco, you will probably need a fifty-pound box of topping mud — the kind painters and tapers use — which can be purchased at any paint store for about nine to ten dollars. It will cover two or three good sized walls. Using a notched, linoleum trowel, fan it on walls for a great "sunrise" effect. Easy — just get top row going in one direction — first, all the way across, and then add each row on opposite arches. See example picture on page 262.

Stucco walls — sunrise effect

You can also put very fine sand in the topping mud, mix well, and, using a flat trowel, spread on walls in (thin coat) circular motion. The effect is a slightly grainy stucco look.

If you mix a small amount of straw into the mud and apply on walls in flat, even strokes, the straw suddenly appears and gives a real adobe look. This is great for family rooms with a country feeling.

Fabric wall covering

Small pine boards (about 1" × 4" × 8") can be wrapped with fabric and the boards nailed to the wall a few feet apart to give depth to an otherwise boring wall. You can even put flat pieces or sheets inside every other space.

FURNITURE FIX-UPS

1. To unify odd pieces of furniture, cover them all in the same fabric.

By using the same fabric on draperies and on one piece of furniture, you get a luxurious look. Rooms will also look bigger when just one pattern is used.

2. The parson's table, designed many years ago by a student at the Parson's School of Design, is versatile, transitional, and always in style.

    It is easy to construct because it has only four straight legs, a top, and side aprons. Built to any size, it is appropriate as a dining room table, desk, night stand, end table, cocktail table, etc. Any chair blends with it. See top right photo.

Parson's Table

3. Two small filing cabinets, topped by a door or wooden plank, make a great kneehole desk. Two sawhorses and a glass top also make a great desk.

265

4. An old sewing machine base can make a great desk or table.

5. A round plywood top (purchased at a lumber store), along with a package of four wooden legs, can make a great table for the living room or bedroom when the table is covered with floor-length cloth.

6. Part of an old iron fence or a gate can make a great headboard.

7. Wood pallets, used for shipping bricks or tile, can even be painted bright colors, stacked two deep, and covered with glass for a cocktail table. Or, stacked two deep and piled high with colorful cushions, they can be used as seating.

8. A canopy bed effect can be created with two panels of draperies attached to the ceiling on each side of the bed. Just screw a piece of 1" × 1" wood to the ceiling each side of the bed, staple the drapery to it, and tie the drapery back.

You can make a canopy bed by stretching a matching sheet over two wooden poles.

9. To brighten old furniture, make lots of toss pillows in complementary colors and place them all over the furniture. You might even use the same fabrics at the windows in shirred draperies.

10. P.V.C. pipe also makes great furniture. Use the elbow joints for corner turns and the straight pieces for sides.

11. An old iron or brass baby crib makes a great day bed. Remove the hinged side, cover the mattress with fabric, and add lots of pillows.

12. Plywood five-sided cubes can be painted or covered with fabric or paper, stacked, and secured to the wall. They make great niches for toys, books, or clothes. Turned with the open end to the floor, they also make handy bunk tables, end tables, or cocktail tables.

13. Drafting lights, fixed to the wall, make great desk lamps or lamps for night tables. They are also great in sporty rooms,

mounted on the wall behind a sofa. You can purchase them in hardware stores for only $16.

14. A simple 12" × 12" square of mirror tile can be painted for a wall hanging. Make a stencil of your child's name, initials, a flower, or a design, tape it on securely, paint on the design, buy an inexpensive metal frame, and you have a great accessory.

15. Small, two-drawer metal or cardboard filing cabinets come in great colors and are handy in a small child's room for clothing storage or in a guest area for extra drawer space.

16. In dull, dingy basement play room with high, obscure windows, mask off floor-to-ceiling letters of the alphabet and paint on the letters in bright colors.

17. Make throw pillows for a child out of cotton bandanas.
18. Sawhorses, painted decorator colors, are great as bases for dining tables (use a door), desks (use a plank), or a console table (use glass top).
19. An old park bench makes a good loveseat.
20. Room sized folding screens covered in fabric and hinged together make great room dividers or backdrops for a sofa or even headboards. Cover the plywood planks (1" × 12" × 72") in fabric or paper and hinge them together with piano hinges.

21. Army cots with foam cushions make great mini-sofas.
22. Industrial metal storage shelving, sprayed with good colors, are great bookshelves or television shelves.
23. Old or new quilts, thrown over a long-skirted round table, make a nostalgic and charming end table or night table.
24. The small 24" cable spools used by telephone and power companies, can be retrieved from them at no cost to you. Cut off one disc, upholster the other with batting and foam, cover the entire spool with fabric, and you have a child's "mushroom" chair.
25. A shelf, placed about 14" or so from the ceiling (just over windows and doors) all the way around the room, conveys a feeling of charm if it is loaded with plants, books, baskets, and other treasures.

ACCESSORIES

1. If an accessory is not beautiful, useful, or meaningful to you, it does not belong in a room.
2. If knobs or handles on cabinets are missing and you can't find replacements, change all the hardware to match. There is nothing worse than sloppy looking cabinets.
3. Cabinets can take on a fresh appearance with just a coat of paint.
4. Cardboard carpet tubes, cut to various lengths and roped together, make a great container for dried flowers or grasses.
5. A collection or inexpensive baskets, assembled on a kitchen or family room wall, makes a great wall grouping.
6. Baskets of potatoes, onions, and vegetables on the kitchen floor or about the sink give the feeling of a warm, gourmet kitchen.
7. Hanging baskets made of wire can hang in a kitchen and hold vegetables, potatoes, and onions, or they can hang in a bathroom and hold towels and soaps.

8. Large squares of colorful fabric or a large scarf stapled on a wooden frame, make great "paintings."
9. Get a large oil (plain) canvas from an art store and get one color of paint for each of your children. Let each child step in their color and walk across the canvas *once* and each in a different direction. It makes a great painting and a family treasure!
10. To camouflage radiators and steam pipes, paint them the same color as the walls.

QUESTIONS MOST FREQUENTLY ASKED ABOUT INTERIOR DESIGN

Q. **What should we start purchasing first? Our budget is limited, and we need a LONG-TERM plan.**

A. A pair of rocking chairs. Start with your background first in this order: floorcoverings, walls, window coverings. If a room is void of furniture but has a pretty background, it is still a pretty room and pleasant to be in. If a room has plain, drab, or garrish floors, walls, windows, and a magnificent costly sofa, it is still an ugly room that will actually detract from the sofa.

Q. **I can understand about backgrounds, but we have nothing to sit on. What can we do to make the room functional besides pretty?**

A. After your backgrounds are completed or during their purchase, buy a secondhand sofa or a pair of chairs for the least money possible. Find sheets that blend with your backgrounds and slipcover the used furniture. A few nice decorator pillows and the furniture will hardly be noticeable.

Q. **How can we coordinate the colors of two adjoining rooms?**

A. Very carefully. Rooms visible to each other must be compatible in color schemes. To do this, adapt the same basic color scheme in each room: one dominant color in one room is adapted as a subdominant color in another. For example, if one room has beige carpet, blue walls, a blue sofa, and navy accents, the other room might have beige carpet, navy walls, a navy sofa, and blue accents.

Q. Our living room is cut up by lots of windows. What do you suggest?

A. Be good to your neighbors! If your windows are exceptionally attractive (cased in wood, small window panes, etc.), paint the walls a bold dark color, and paint the window moldings white or cream. Then don't install draperies. If you have a privacy or sun problem, add tight-fitting heat control roller shades which can be installed in recessed areas.

If your windows are a high ranch style, you might consider small louvered shutters painted the lightest color in your room. Or if they are massive and fill large areas of wall space, don't hang yards and yards of fabric as it will diminish the room size and the view. Instead, try bamboo roller shades, Roman shades, folding fabric screens, or vertical louvers.

Q. How can I combine patterns? I love the look of two or three prints used together.

A. Patterns should share common colors. Only one pattern should dominate, but its dominance should derive from the amount used and not from the size of the pattern. They should all be approximately the same scale (size of print), although this is not a hard and fast rule.

Q. What is the best use of space when two children share a bedroom?

A. First, streamline the room. Remove draperies, busy prints, and all other fixtures or obtrusive items. Use mini-blinds at the windows, small prints, and plain carpet. Two twin beds can be used as an "L" in the corner or put end-to-end on one wall as a day bed or sofa or stacked as bunkbeds or trundle bed. Use built-ins or move dressers into the closets (redesign hanging space), and use the area above the windows and around the upper part of the room for shelf area to store seldom-used toys, etc. If these ideas aren't acceptable, sell one child.

Q. **Our dining room is a small area in the living room, and we always feel crowded when we eat there. What can we do?**

A. Eat more salads. Mirror the end wall as it will give the illusion of more space. Choose smaller-scaled furniture and avoid heavy or completely upholstered chairs. Avoid a fussy and elaborate chandelier and choose light colors, wood, and fabrics.

Q. **My husband likes one style, and I like another. How can we best combine our two tastes?**

A. Move him into the garage. If you stay with an eclectic look, which is a mix or collected look, both tastes can usually be combined around a neutral color scheme. Choose simply-styled upholstery pieces and add his chrome and glass cocktail table and your Eighteenth Century sofa table, etc.

Q. **There is a room in our house that has very little natural light. It is dark in the middle of the day. What can we do to make it look lighter?**

A. Paint the walls a very light color — eggshell or off-white. Eliminate as much drapery and window covering as possible, use mini-blinds installed inside the window frame. If you use a roller shade or Roman shade, install them above the window area so that when pulled up, the maximum amount of window is exposed. Keep the floors and furniture as light in color as possible. Avoid placing large pieces in front of or near the windows. Large pieces in the room can also deflect needed light.

Avoid dark or gloomy colors, patterns, or prints of any kind. If you try all this and the room is still dark, lie down and take a nap.

Q. Our house has seemed to shrink as the children have grown older. What can we do for storage space? (This is a question often asked by single adults living in or sharing a small apartment.)

A. Seriously, give Deseret Industries a call. If you give yourself a few days of cleaning and evaluating, you will probably be surprised at how much you have accumulated that could be discarded or given away. I know those boxes of empty baby food jars, flip top tabs, all of Johnny's shoes he ever wore (He's now 21.), your husband's old fishing gear, and the tennis racket with no strings all have useful purposes. But perhaps not in this life. Be discriminating. You can't save all the shells on the beach so pick only the best and most valuable. Redesign closets and try to figure out a better way to rearrange the shelf and closet areas. Consolidate as much as possible. For example, perhaps two similar items can share a common drawer or cabinet. Also, you might use items like keepsakes, towels, dishes, quilts, etc., for decorative display rather than keeping them stored in a closet or drawer.

SOME MORE TIPS

1. Protect fabrics and furniture from the sun by keeping them away from windows with direct and hot sun.
2. Use a reputable dry cleaner and not Sam's Specials.
3. Vacuum often to remove dust.
4. Remove spots immediately.
5. Remember, very few fabrics are washable.
6. Fabrics are not made to last forever so choose heavier ones for stress areas and Scotchguard every six months.

7. In children's rooms and play areas, buy cheap carpet as it will wear out from soil and stains before it will wear out from wear. (Put the plush ones in the master bedroom or living room.)
8. If possible, don't allow food in carpeted areas.
9. Reverse the rugs in a room for more wear.
10. Buy home furnishings from reputable dealers. There is no such thing as "wholesale to the public." You get what you pay for. Dealers mark up their products to live — they have nothing to give away. True sales are a real bargain, however, so watch reputable dealers for their sales.
11. Get informed. Local, county extension services can provide you with information on how to shop for quality and good buys.
12. If possible, work with a professional designer. They are not out to get you, and they are expert in budgeting money. You must be honest and up front with them about how much money you have to spend versus your needs. They know sources, and they know how to rob Peter to pay Paul. They can stretch your dollar farther than you can. If your budget is very small — pennies — and you approach a designer and they are stupid enough to refuse you, keep shopping until you find one who won't refuse you. Recently, I completed a home with a budget of $75,000. They were a couple who had come to me three years earlier to help them with a bathroom and the wallpapering of two bedrooms. He was just starting out in life, but in three years he had been very successful. They came back to me, not only because they liked my talent, but because I had treated them no differently than anyone else, even if it was only for a few dollars worth of wallpaper. If a designer is intimidating, it's their loss and your gain. Go find one who is ethical and honest.

However, look for credentials. Don't get involved with Hilda Housewife or the sleezy looking "decorator" store on the corner. There are a lot of people "decorating" who are not reputable either financially or in ability. A good credential is A.S.I.D. after their name. The American Society of Interior Designers is a professional society of designers with a national membership of about 15,000. They subscribe to a strict code of ethics. Members must pass a rigid examination that includes everything from ability with colors to financial expertise regarding clients. Also, check with your Better Business Bureau. For A.S.I.D. members near you, write to A.S.I.D. National Headquarters, 730 Fifth Avenue, New York, New York 10019.

Before

After

No matter how poor you are, what your budget is like, or where you reside, your home should be a pleasant place in which to live. It should reflect your spirit, personality, talents, and love — love not only for family and friends but that love which is RESPECT and REVERENCE for the beauty of the world. The Lord made this world with *great* love and respect. He adorned it with beauty, using His creative powers and skills. He loves exquisite things — they stem from His talents. Can you strive for anything less?

A can of paint, a fresh flower, a family picture, a green plant, a colorful pillow carefully chosen and arranged can mean the difference between a hovel and a palace. It doesn't matter if you live in a shack, just look around, LIFE UP your eyes, and see the potential. Remember that "two men looked out from prison bars. One saw the mud, the other saw the stars."

Find those stars and then carefully, with great LOVE and POWER, let them light up your dwelling. Acknowledge the fact that you are really preparing a place for the Savior.

Chapter  Seven

Your Mirror Image

"And I, God, created man in mine own image."
—*Moses 2:27*

The photograph on the front of this book says so many personal things from me to you. I won't tell you everything that went through my mind as I chose this photograph over all the others, but I hope your eyes will linger over its color, its lines, its softness, and mostly, over its feeling. A woman's physical countenance is a reflection of her inner self. The physical and the inner woman are inseparable. The lovely young ballerina's reflection could mirror either success or defeat. Her form is such that I can see much self-discipline in that pose. Her mirror image reflects her thoughts. A woman will never become anything she does not think about.

Johnny Lingo was the sharpest trader in all the islands. He knew value. Johnny Lingo was respected for his shrewdness. After many months of being away, Johnny returned to his native village to negotiate a most interesting bargain — the purchase of a wife.

The villagers gathered quickly as Johnny's large canoe came to shore. Before long the whole island was in an uproar. They had learned that he was going to ask Mahana's father for her hand in marriage. Mahana was skinny and shy and had a "face like a stone." Johnny could have had any woman on the whole island; why did he choose her?

The rumor was that he wanted her because she was so ugly that he could get her for nothing. According to custom, he would offer the father a cow or perhaps two for the hand of his daughter. The more cows a bridegroom paid, the more beautiful and valuable was the woman. As tongues wagged and people snickered, poor Mahana fled from the scene. For two or three cows, a man could buy a very nice wife. For four or five he could buy a beauty. (Five cows was the most ever paid for a wife in those islands.) Her father would have taken a three-legged cow to be rid of her! She was humiliated and hid in the bushes near her home.

Johnny Lingo came through the clearing and stood in front of the hut. A crowd pressed near, straining to hear every word.

"I ask for Mahana's hand in marriage. What price do you say?"

Her father paused, he was under great pressure. He consulted his uncle, an adviser, because he was afraid to ask too much or too little. The uncle convinced him to ask for a high price.

"Three cows!" Mahana's father said.

It took nearly five minutes for the crowd to stop laughing. In fact, they may have been laughing still when Johnny raised his hand for silence.

"Three cows," he said, "that is many, but not enough for Mahana. I will give you eight cows."

There was silence. It was as if everyone on the whole island had quit breathing. EIGHT COWS! They were stunned!

As the crowd quietly dispersed, Johnny said that he would return in the morning with the cows.

Morning came and still Mahana would not come forward.

She did not believe he would keep his word, but before long eight fat cows were marched directly to her father's front door, and Johnny Lingo tenderly claimed his wife.

The afternoon of the wedding festival, he paid a visit to the storekeeper to purchase a gift for his bride. The storekeeper questioned him about the necessity of giving eight cows for Mahana. Wasn't Johnny the sharpest trader in all the islands? Surely he could have made a better bargain?

"When they talk of marriage contracts," Johnny replied, "it will always be remembered that Johnny Lingo paid eight cows for his wife."

So that was it! He was vain, mused the storekeeper, just a poor vain fool.

Many months passed, and one morning the storekeeper heard that Johnny and Mahana were back from their honeymoon. They had been gone much longer than expected. The storekeeper decided to pay them a visit and bring Johnny the gift he had ordered.

When he entered their house, he could not believe what he saw! Instead of a skinny, shy, and homely girl, he found a confident, elegant, and very lovely woman. She greeted him with graciousness and then excused herself to collect water.

"Johnny, I can't believe that that's Mahana. She is so *lovely!* What happened?" he asked.

"I have loved her since we were children," he said. "She was always lovely." Then Johnny explained how badly a woman must feel when she is bargained for by her husband as he hopes to get the *lowest* price. Later, the women boast to one another about the number of cows that were given for them.

"Can you imagine," said Johnny, "how lowly a woman who has been traded for one or two cows must feel? Mahana will never feel that way."

"I misjudged you," said the storekeeper. "I thought you paid

283

eight cows to look good in the eyes of your friends. I didn't know you wanted to make Mahana happy."

Then Johnny Lingo said something so simple, yet so masterful and so powerful that if you truly understood it, your life would move boldly forward.

"I didn't just want to make her happy. I wanted her to BE an eight-cow woman. There are many things that can make a woman beautiful, but the most important of all is what she thinks of herself!"

In other words, YOU HAVE GOT TO BELIEVE IN YOURSELF.

In her father's home, Mahana had been made to feel ugly and worthless. Yet when she was *literally* the most valuable woman on the island, she felt her great worth, and she thought those thoughts that made her become beautiful.

You are *literally* a noble woman, a daughter of the Most High. You have got to believe in yourself. You will never become anything you don't think about for "as a man thinketh so is he." You won't ever become a god if you don't begin to think and act like one.

If you think you are ugly, unattractive, shy, deformed, poor, fat, or sloppy, that's all you will ever be! You must begin to believe in yourself and to say to yourself: "I am lovely. I am a daughter of a king. I won't stay fat. I can look better. I can succeed. I'm worth it! I AM WORTH IT!" You will become exactly the woman you believe you are. I promise you.

Apathy breeds apathy. YOU HAVE GOT TO CARE. YOU MUST BELIEVE IN WHO YOU ARE. Your Heavenly Father loves you. He knows where you are and what your address is. He wants all of his daughters to KNOW they are eight-cow women and more! He wants to help you. He knows how hard it is to battle Satan. *He did it.* He made it. He is a success, and when you and I left the pre-existence, we, too, were destined for success. WE WERE BORN TO SUCCEED. The world is looking to you. You are needed so very much.

So what keeps you from success? What is it that keeps you on a certain level, not seeming to go forward or backward?

About a year and a half ago I had an unusual experience while reading my patriarchal blessing. A line that I had read many times for over twenty years suddenly "jumped" out at me and took on a whole new meaning. It was a great promise for a most sacred blessing, perhaps the greatest that I could ever hope for in mortal life. I was stunned. How COULD I HAVE MISSED THIS ALL THESE YEARS? As I focused again on the sentence, the meaning and an admonition to work harder at my personal program were confirmed by the power of the Holy Ghost. I wondered why it had taken all these years for me to see the meaning in that sentence.

Two months passed and the same thing happened again with another line in my blessing! Again I wondered why I hadn't seen the significance earlier.

During the next year seven distinct and most important revelations were given to me regarding my patriarchal blessing. Each time I questioned why the Lord had seen fit to reveal such things to me. I wondered why He had withheld them from me for so many years.

Several months later I took my patriarchal blessing apart, line by line. At the top of the page I wrote:

My Patriarchal Blessing

I then wrote down "Lineage" and underneath that I wrote every sentence in the paragraph that dealt with my lineage and birthright.

Then I wrote down four headings: (1) Warnings, (2) Counsel, (3) Gifts, and (4) Promises.

Line by line I entered everything in my blessing under one of those columns. It was more difficult than I had assumed it would be. To determine differences between counsel and warnings, gifts and promises, took exactness and listening to the Spirit. The whole task took two evenings. When I had concluded, I had only two warnings, half a page of counsel, half a page of gifts, and nearly a whole page of promises.

I was intrigued at what lay before me. My premortal personality seemed to unfold before me, and I suddenly realized that the Lord was talking to a woman He *really* knew. Here was exact counsel for a specific person. However, the real lesson came a few days later as I looked over the list again. My eyes seemed to linger over the column marked "counsel," and the most sobering realization became suddenly clear. A voice seemed to be telling me: "It isn't that the Lord didn't *want* to give you those revelations, that knowledge. He couldn't. He was bound. Anita, you didn't live up to your part of the bargain. You didn't pay the price." I recalled this passage from the Doctrine and Covenants:

"I, the Lord, am bound when ye do what I say; but when ye do not what I say, ye have no promise" (D&C 82:10).

As I deliberated over these thoughts and events, I asked myself when it was that I had determined to lengthen my stride, to recommit myself to the gospel; was it when I had begun to submit myself to the whole will of the Lord?

After pondering that in my heart, I knew that it had been about three years previous to that time. The thoughts began to swell. It had taken three years — three years to let myself know that I was serious about obeying *all* of His commandments. It wasn't that I was more righteous or closer to perfection. All those who know me will attest to that! No, it wasn't perfection, it was commitment — a decision to succeed.

When you are on the Lord's terms, then He can help. If you want His support to lose weight and you continue to eat, you will find that support quite distant. If you are in debt and keep spending, how can He help you? If you need self-control and pray for it but continue to avoid a concentrated effort, you will find frustration. He will bless you and help you, but you have to live up to your half of the bargain!

Your Heavenly Father loves you. He KNOWS you. He knows your FULL potential. He has given you the gifts, the counsel, the warnings, the powers to achieve that FULL potential. The promises are that He will continue to help you and that if you but STRIVE to do His will, you will have all that He has. He knows that each woman is priceless. If you will just do what He says — at least STRIVE to obey ALL of His commandments — He will not leave you comfortless. He WANTS to give you much knowledge and many treasures. He has promised that "all saints who remember to keep and do these sayings, walking in obedience to the commandments, shall receive health in their navel and marrow to their bones; and shall find wisdom and great treasures of knowledge, *even hidden treasures*" (D&C 89:18-19, italics added).

Such is the Lord's promise regarding the Word of Wisdom. Personal health and hygiene are important aspects of the counsel which the Lord has given us. Respect, love, and honor for your body are spiritual matters. *Therefore, spiritual direction and aid can come to you in governing your body and environment.* However, if you have neglected your physical appearance or steeped your home in disorder because of a lack of self-discipline, the Lord cannot promise to help you. But when you turn your heart, commit yourself to do it right, and "give place," He will help you and inspire you. HE WILL, AND YOU CAN!

The hard part is the stick-to-itiveness that you need to put the physical you in complete order. Personal grooming of self and environment can only lead you from a poor self-image to a more noble one. You must ACT worthy of yourself. Satan knows that, so he will discourage you or tell you it isn't worth it, that you aren't worth it, or that it doesn't matter. It does matter!

I asked for letters from sisters who read the first book in this series so that I might gather "attitudes" for future books and lectures.

One warm, winter afternoon a letter came from a loving woman in Salt Lake City. She had read my book one night and then had been impressed to go to her journal and read the entries for the past year. There on the pages of her journal were the *same* thoughts and feelings that were written in my book. This is what she wrote to me: "You've crystallized my philosophies succinctly. I got out my journal and reviewed this past year's entries, and I was brought to humility . . . because I realized the Lord loves all His children alike, and He will give the *same* true answers, impressions, and peace to any faithful seeker."

You see, we are the same in that we share the same feelings of *hope* and *excellence*. God is constant and speaks the same truth to each woman who seeks it. If you seek, He will help. He wants you to be a success. You were born to succeed.

Whenever there is a pursuit of excellence, there will be challenges. Challenges to be set are challenges to be met. Each woman can best determine her own useful goals and challenges, but I would like to personally challenge you to certain levels of excellence. Consider this as being just between you and me. Write to me, tell me your successes, your failures. I CARE. I KNOW THE WOMAN GOD INTENDED YOU TO BE. I want you to succeed. If you don't have a mortal friend in the world, you do now — me. Remember, though, that it is your immortal friend that will help you through any darkness.

I CHALLENGE YOU!

1. PRAY. Pray every morning and every night. Pray to a *real* person. Ask Him to help you gain self-control and become more organized. Do not miss both prayers a day for a period of three months. Then, after the three months, set

another goal for six months. After six months, increase your goal to one year and so on until you become perfect in prayer. You will see the change. I promise you.

2. CONTROL. Control your appetite for one day, being careful to record every item that goes into your mouth. Wait a few days and then control your appetite for one week. At the end of the week, double it and use control for two weeks. Continue to double the goal until you are in full control again. Make a commitment never to be fat again. Start your endurance exercise plan for one week and then do it for two. Continue to double the weeks until you have learned to love it!

3. MAINTAIN. Maintain your desirable weight for three months. If you must, go on a diet and the endurance exercise program to lose the weight first, then maintain that weight for three months (again doubling the goal each time it is reached).

4. USE MAKE-UP. Take the techniques described in this book and use them daily for two weeks. At the end of the two weeks, re-evaluate and if you don't seem to have a better attitude, if you haven't received more compliments, if your appearance hasn't been enhanced, then you can alter the process. I know it will be one of the greatest treatments for your self-esteem, and it will be a new look for you. You must promise to do it faithfully for two weeks. (Consult a cosmetic counselor for thorough help.)

5. STUDY. Study your body type. Stand in front of a full-length mirror for twenty minutes and write down all the pluses and minuses about your body. Evaluate whether your neck is short, your legs are long, your waist too high, etc., and write it all down.

6. EVALUATE. Evaluate your torso versus your wardrobe. Dispose of all long, flowering mumus with puffy sleeves (unless you save them for the ward luau). Dispose of all clothes that make you look like a three-year-old child (pink rose buds, little baby gingham, etc.). Recycle all you can. Ask yourself how you can improve your physical appearance through your clothes. Write down the ideas that come to you.

7. CONCENTRATE. Concentrate on organizing your wardrobe with a new level of dignity and femininity. Start a plan to slowly acquire more flattering style for your torso (as fast as your budget permits).

8. VISIT. Visit a good hairdresser and get a decent haircut. Learn how to keep your hair in good condition. Never let it get greasy.

9. CONCERN. Concern yourself with the organization of your home. Ask yourself: Am I making the most of my time? What is my greatest problem? List priorities to get your home in order.

10. CLEAN. Clean your home and keep it clean. Take one month to thoroughly clean your house. From your list of priorities, clean first from the worst job to the least offensive. Challenge your family to help you. Even the little ones can do something. Keep your house clean for one more month. Each time double the goal. Use helps from this book or other books if necessary. Ask a friend to help you. JUST DO IT!

11. DEVELOP. Develop your personality in your home. Try to develop a plan whereby you can add wallpaper, frame a family picture, hang a green plant or something *each month* to make your home a more cheerful and happy place.

12. TEACH. Teach your children that one of the greatest responsibilities they have for good self-esteem is a pleasant, personal appearance and environment.

Take my challenges, alter or reword them to suit you, add your own, but please, take the challenge. They are outlined to allow you to start a new one each month. You are only twelve challenges away from a better and happier YOU! Perhaps your situation won't allow all twelve this year — do six this year and six next year, but please START NOW.

These challenges are spiritual and are related to all those other challenges you have set for yourself. The victories over genealogy and scripture reading and tithe paying and so on are all related to the challenges I have described. It is part of a TOTAL PACKAGE.

What happens if you try and try and then fail? Remember not to stop at the August of your life. You just don't know how much stronger you may be in September!

Let me share with you a letter from an athlete named Cliff Cushman. He won the Silver Medal for the 400 meter hurdles in the 1960 Olympics and was a top candidate for the Gold Medal in the 1964 Olympics. However, in the American trials, he hit and tripped over a hurdle and was eliminated. The letter was in reply to hundreds of messages of sympathy:

> Over fifteen years ago I saw a star, first place in the Olympic games. I literally started to run after it. In 1960, I came within three yards of grabbing it. This year, I stumbled, fell, and watched it recede four more years away.
>
> In a split second, all the many years of training, pain, sweat, blisters, and agony of running were simply wiped out.
>
> BUT I TRIED! I would much rather fail

knowing I had put forth an HONEST effort than
to never have tried at all.

Certainly I was very disappointed falling flat
on my face, however, there is nothing I can
do now but get up, pick the cinders from my
wounds, and take one more step — followed
by one more — and one more — until the
steps turn into miles and the miles into
Success!

That is exactly how it is done — a little at a time, steps to
miles and miles to successes. Nevertheless, you must set the steps
just a little out of reach. *Unless your reach exceeds your grasp, how
can you be sure what you can attain?*

Step by step the spirit of the Lord will be there to comfort,
counsel, and encourage you if you will but acknowledge and seek
for that help. When your self-esteem suffers, the joy in your heart
diminishes. The world seems somewhat duller, and the unsettled
feeling deep in your bosom disturbs your sense of peace. It is
peace we seek. Peace! We cry, and we hope it comes. Yet it is not
in the darkness of the night but in the first dim rays of dawn —
the dawn of a new day, the dawn of a *renewed* relationship with
the Holy Ghost. He is the Comforter. No matter how dark the
night, the dawn is irresistible! And, like the dawn that always
comes, the Savior is always there waiting for us to come out of
that darkness and solitude of a less than godlike course. He is
there with open arms if you will just listen for that voice — the
mediator who comes in a soft but reassuring voice. Are you
listening? Do you hear the counsel, the advice, the encouragement? That small voice speaks to you and tells you that you are a
daughter of God worthy of nobility, born to succeed, and that
you can and must ACT worthy of yourself. Then as you kneel in
tender reverence and humble prayer, your eyes fill with tears and

you whisper that you know He lives, that He cares. You express your love for Him and for His son, and you tell Him of your gratitude for the gift of the Holy Ghost.

Then, by a voice which tells you in your mind and in your heart, you are given to know that our Heavenly Father loves you.

That is JOY! That is PEACE! That is SELF-ESTEEM!

God *knows* you. He knows where you live. He cares about you. You were born to succeed. No, it is much more than that. You were *elected* to succeed. The beautiful woman which He intends for you to become — the goddess — is but a reverence and mirror image away.

You must *reflect* and thereby *rise* to that election.

THE WOMEN'S ENRICHMENT SERIES

Self-Esteem and the Physical You deals with the physical aspects of each woman's self-esteem. It is the second book in the series on self-esteem, the other books in the series being: *Self-Esteem and the Latter-day Saint Woman,* a spiritual philosophy meant to encourage you to seek out the divine within you, and forthcoming works, *Self-Esteem and the Social You* and *Self-Esteem for the Latter-day Saint Youth.* These are books which discuss relationships with husbands, parents, children, friends, etc. Talents, fears, manners, opportunities, needs, desires, charity, and other matters are all focused upon. The last book in the series will be *Voices From My Sisters,* a book of the letters written to me by Latter-day Saint women. It is hoped that the book will give sisters in Maine, Tennessee, etc., an opportunity of hearing of the thoughts and feelings of sisters in California, Idaho, etc. These letters will, of course, be published anonymously — you can even write anonymously if you wish. I need to hear from you. I need to feel your spirit and cares, failures and successes, plans and goals, and whatever else you need to "discuss." You also need to hear from each other to see that you are not different from anyone else.

Please feel free to write to me. You are my friends, and I love you.

Anita Canfield
5895 West Patrick Lane
Las Vegas, Nevada 89118

If you would like to subscribe to a monthly newsletter co-published by Anita Canfield and Scott Zimmerman, Ph.D., send your name, address, and $4.00 for a one-year subscription to cover typesetting, printing, postage, etc., to:

NEWSLETTER
946 East Sahara Avenue
Las Vegas, Nevada 89104

The newsletter will contain monthly spiritual messages, fashion and make-up tips, a weight control and exercise spot by Dr. and Mrs. Zimmerman, and a question and answer section. Please send your questions or problems that you would like answered to the same address. These will be published anonymously but with city and state.